Willy Brandt
a portrait
of the German Chancellor

a portrait
of the German Chancellor

with 28 photographs and 3 facsimiles

HERMANN OTTO BOLESCH
HANS DIETER LEICHT

Willy Brandt

a portrait
of the
German Chancellor

HORST ERDMANN VERLAG
Tübingen and Basel

TRANSLATED BY ALICE DENES

Contents

List of Illustrations

Foreword

"In the last 24 years much has been done and achieved but past performances will no longer count in future. It did not please everyone yesterday and will do so less tomorrow," said President Gustav Heinemann after being sworn in on July 1st, 1969. He then went on to say : "We have to improve on our achievements. Social change progresses, and so it is up to all of us to realize the constitution's call for the *building up of social democracy* by increasing our efforts. We shall have to see to it that the individual's freedom is protected not only from the power of the State but equally from economic and social forces. Time and again the influence of the organisations and their lobbyists runs counter to our order in which privileges, though abolished by law, still exist in social reality."

"We must grow into a society of achievement of growth and education in which freedom for all shall be brought about by giving to each his real and personal opportunity. The challenge is not less but more democracy, that is the grand goal to which all of us and the young especially have to pledge ourselves."

"There are some difficult countries. One of them is Germany. But it is our home land. We live and work here. So we wish to make our contribution to one and indivisible humanity by means of and through this country."

The minutes of the fifth session in the sixth election period to the German *Bundestag* record on pages 20 to 34 the Government Declaration of October 28, 1969, which Chancellor Brandt concluded with these words :

"In recent years some people in this country have feared that the second German Democratic State might go the way of the first. I never believed that. Today I believe it less than ever.

"No—we are not at the end of our Democracy, we are only just beginning. We want to be and become a people of good neighbours, both at home and abroad."

The German government that took power in 1969 declared through its Chancellor :

"This government pays lip service to no-one. It sets high standards not only for others but also for itself. It lays down concrete objectives. These objectives can be achieved only if the citizen's relationship to his State and his government changes quite a bit. In a democracy a government can be successful only if it is supported by the *democratic commitment of the citizens...*

"We do not seek admirers; we need people who critically share with us the thinking, the decisions and the responsibility."

As Federal Chancellor, Willy Brandt is putting into effect what he describes as the contrast of living democracy to merely static or formal democracy, i.e. the kind of democracy that regards the citizen exclusively or predominantly as a man with a vote.

The new style Brandt has introduced in the leadership of the Social Democratic Party of Germany is something quite different from what professional technicians occasionally have tried to make of it. The secret of this new style is direct contact with his fellow citizens, the intimate dialogue with the people, the participation of everyone in the discussion of matters that actually concern him.

The important thing to Brandt, and about Brandt, is that he has persisted and not given in about matters that seemed crucial to him. In consequence he can justly say :

"The self-confidence of this government will be reflected in its tolerance. It will appreciate the kind of solidarity expressed in criticism. We are not chosen people, we are elected. So we shall seek a dialogue with all who care for this Democracy."

Through difficult years Willy Brandt represented, influenced and developed German policy in the most difficult place in the divided Germany, Berlin. Through difficult years he forged the Socialist Party into the leading political force in Germany. As Foreign Minister he gained moral and political credit for his country.

Brandt's dictum "We wish to be and become a people of good

neighbours, both at home and abroad" is the best resolution for this nation which must make peace with itself and help to secure peace in Europe which is growing closer in the world.

I may be permitted to refer once more to President Heinemann's speech of July 1, 1969 in which he said :

"Our democratic order of a philosophically neutral State is a tremendous opportunity. It settles such practical community questions as can be put to the vote by majority decisions. Democratic relations require the willingness to compromise. However, the questions of what is good and fine, questions of truth and faith, not being votable are referred by our order to the method of the dialogue and placed in the charge of tolerance.

"The other day I recalled a word by Emerson : 'God gives everyone the choice between truth and sleep. Take which you like. You cannot have both'."

Herbert Wehner

The Chancellor is the Man who Matters

All eyes are fixed on Willy Brandt, as he sits on the SPD front bench in the *Bundestag* 81 long-winded minutes have been consumed by the formal procedure of roll-call and balloting for the new Federal Chancellor. Another twenty minutes for counting the votes. Now the crucial moment has arrived.

A secretary hands the results to *Bundestag* President Kai Uwe von Hassel. The murmur in the benches and the galleries dies down. The sudden quiet has the effect of a sound failure on TV. The minute hand on the wall clock jumps to 11.21 a.m. Von Hassel rises to announce the results of the secret ballot :

"Votes cast 495; ayes 251; nays 235; voided votes 4; abstentions 5."

Before a hand can move, he continues :

"According to Article 63, Para 2 of the Constitution, the elected Chancellor is he who receives the majority of *Bundestag* members' votes. The absolute majority of deputies eligible to vote is 248. I therefore confirm that Willy Brandt, the deputy nominated by the Federal President, has received the majority of the votes. I am asking Deputy Brandt : Do you accept the vote?"

Willy Brandt has risen. Without hesitation, loudly and firmly, he says :.

"Yes, Herr President, I do."

For a fraction of a second there is complete silence. Then a springflood of applause erupts on the benches of the SPD and allied FDP, bringing many of the deputies to their feet, cheering. The jubilation spreads over to the galleries. A good many visitors too clap their hands enthusiastically. Rut Brandt's face is radiant with relief and happiness.

On the floor of the house fellow party members crowd around

1

Willy Brandt to shake his hand. The Opposition too has sent its wellwishers. And of course the FDP which has just demonstrated its loyalty for the second time, the first time having been Gustav Heinemann's election as President eight months previously.

One moment of this memorable hour was of Herbert Wehner stepping up to Brandt and the two men embracing in sudden emotion, firmly and affectionately. The grand old man of the Social Democrats and their younger hero. It was Herbert Wehner's big refurbishing of 1959 that first cleared the way for the SPD to become a great people's party. The following year, in 1960, Wehner had swept Willy Brandt through against all party resistance as candidate for the Chancellorship. Now, a decade later, a daring move has reaped triumph and victory.

Brandt's election as fourth *Bundeskanzler* on this 21st October, 1969 opens a new chapter in the history of Germany. For the first time in 39 years a Social Democrat has taken the helm of a German government. The international press speaks of a "changing of the Watch on the Rhine", a "new beginning in Germany", a "historic turning point".

History loves a coincidence. Also on this triumphal day for a Socialist Chancellor it has provided one. 91 years before to the day, on October 21, 1878, Bismarck had pushed through his pet Act banning Social Democracy as a "threat to the public"...

With three votes, Brandt's majority was a slender one. But it immediately brought back memories of 1949 when Konrad Adenauer barely squeezed through his first election as Chancellor— with the help of his own vote.

"I am contented," said Brandt after being elected. "I'm grateful for the trust placed in me and a little proud to hold this high office."

And who was to blame him for being "a little proud"? He had attempted the leap to Palais Schaumburg twice, and failed. In 1961 he was defeated by Adenauer, in 1965 by Ludwig Erhard. After that second futile bid he had considered resigning his candidacy for Chancellor. The blows below the belt of that campaign had taken their toll. Embittered, disillusioned and deeply hurt, Brandt had retired to Berlin. At the time he said he supposed that governing mayor was his job and Berlin his place. One had better not count on him as candidate for the Chancellorship in 1969.

2

A severe crisis occurred in Brandt's health; he felt he had come to the brink, standing, as he later recalled, 'on the thin line between this life and something else'.

He surmounted the crisis. The scars of the 1965 campaign began to heal. The SPD made him feel that it needed its chairman. At the Dortmund Party Conference of 1966, it again placed him at its helm. A new Willy Brandt had emerged, self-assured, more mature and harder. The biggest and most traditional party in Germany could not have wished for a better leader.

With the formation of the Grand Coalition of Christian Democrats and Social Democrats on December 1, 1966, Brandt became Minister of Foreign Affairs and Vice Chancellor, thus finally moving into the front rank of German politicians. For the first time in West German history, nine Social Democrats became Ministers (out of 19).

"Those who have a sense of history," said Willy Brandt after being sworn in as Foreign Minister, "will not take lightly the fact that a man of my origins and conviction has become German Foreign Minister."

Since Konrad Adenauer's death Brandt has been the best-known German political figure abroad. He is respected by the leaders of nations, esteemed and trusted everywhere. Statesmen and diplomats have described him as the best Foreign Minister Germany ever had.

In the autumn of 1969, after yet another rough election campaign, Brandt had dared to make his third bid for power. "What matters most?—The Chancellor!" had been the CDU slogan coined for Kurt Georg Kiesinger, Premier of the Grand Coalition. "The Chancellor matters most, and so, let our Willy have a go!" countered the Socialists confidently. Their own election slogan promised the voters : "We will build the modern Germany. We have the right men!"

They did have the right man. On the dramatic election night of September 28, while Kiesinger was being toasted as victor, Willy Brandt seized power, looking neither left nor right. Just before midnight he stepped before the TV cameras at Bonn's drab SPD headquarters, which are aptly called "the Barracks", to announce his decision to form the new government with the combined

3

majority of SPD and FDP. "Willy Brandt," a German daily commented, "has grabbed the famous cloak of history and hung on."

The Socialists' takeover, considered overdue by many, but first conceived as possible by Brandt, was completed 23 days later with the Chancellor's election. Brandt moved into Palais Schaumburg, the *Bundeskanzler*'s official residence, as the man laying down the guidelines of German policy on the threshold to a new decade.

Just five months later, on March 19, 1970, the Chancellor travelled to the other German state. His Erfurt meeting with GDR Premier Willi Stoph—'the first inter-German summit conference since 1946'—opened the dialogue with the East German government. In his Government Declaration of October 28, 1969 Brandt had said: "Twenty years after the setting up of the Federal Republic of Germany and the German Democratic Republic we must avert a further estrangement within the German nation; that is, we must try by way of an ordered parallel existence to achieve a common existence."

The Chancellor went to Erfurt without illusions. It was plain to him that no more than an exchange of views could be possible. Yet it was a beginning.

He turned to Bonn profoundly moved. "My brief trip to Erfurt," he said in the *Bundestag* the next day, "was, apart from all else, a strong human experience. That applies especially to my encounter with our countrymen who live in the GDR. It has become manifest— and you will understand if I say no more—that it is not fiction but reality if yesterday in Erfurt I spoke again of the lasting and living reality of a German nation."

His election as Chancellor marked the greatest and proudest day in the life of Willy Brandt, 55 years old, married, father of one daughter and three sons. An extraordinary life it has been. The long march of Willy Brandt began in the Baltic seaport of Lübeck; it led across frontiers and eras, to the depths and to the heights. He himself says: "I have not had an easy life. I've had to make my own way. I have made mistakes and I have learned."

The very fact that Brandt's life progressed in a different way from that of most of his countrymen was exploited by political

4

adversaries and personal enemies for slander and wild rumours about his past. Brandt and his friends had a tough struggle to break down the wall of prejudice and doubt, of malice and defamation.

There may have been error and confusion in his turbulent past, but he has nothing to hide.

"If I had to start all over again," he once confessed, "I would approach things from the same attitude and philosophy."

The "New" Willy Brandt

Since becoming West Germany's Chancellor, Brandt has had to change his mode of life. He had been known as a hard-working politician before, but the special duties of the Chancellorship forced an additional work load upon him. To the surprise of many friends and aides, Brandt easily got into his new routine.

He used to be known as a late starter who was best left alone in the morning, and who got into his real stride only after the sun had gone down. "I am a man who starts the day slowly," he said when he was governing mayor. His staff members of those days would say: "In the morning he's grumpy, after lunch alert and in the evening thoroughly charming."

Brandt, the Chancellor, rises at 7 a.m. At breakfast he reads the morning papers and the *Nachrichtenspiegel,* a news-sheet compiled by the *Bundespresseamt* and delivered to the Chancellor's home by courier. On his way to Palais Schaumburg, where he is driven by a Mercedes 300 SE bearing the Chancellor's licence plate 0–2, he studies papers and makes preliminary notes.

On his desk on the first floor of the Chancellery, a file with the latest and most important telegrams from German ambassadors abroad lies waiting. When Brandt has studied them, he holds a morning conference called *"Lage",* or situation. Usually beginning at 8.30 a.m., this daily conference—nicknamed "morning prayers" —takes place in the Small Cabinet Room. It is attended by Brandt's closest associates in the Chancellery. Here policy is planned and due decisions prejudged. The remainder of the Chancellor's working day is determined by the points on his schedule.

Three times a week the SPD chairman drives to 'the Barracks', party headquarters in Erich-Ollenhauer Street. Even as Chancellor Brandt gives a fair share of his time to party affairs. If the regular

Thursday sessions of the party presidium, over which he presides, draw out over lunch, Brandt has some food brought from the canteen and asks friends to share it with him.

When Brandt's son Peter was younger he once asked rather reproachfully why his daddy did not have a 'proper' job like other fathers who leave home at 8 a.m. and come home at tea-time.

The Chancellor usually gets home in the early evening. Bonn protocol spares him all invitations to cocktail parties, national holiday receptions and diplomatic banquets. At home, Brandt watches TV with his family (when there is anything special on), talks about family matters and enjoys a family dinner. Visitors are rare.

Until bedtime, which is sometimes as early as 11 p.m., he reads and works in his study. He makes notes by hand with a black felt-tipped pen.

There has been much speculation about the "new" Willy Brandt, owing both to his changed regime and to his discipline in the Chancellor's harness. Brandt himself dislikes any fuss about his person. He drily comments : "That kind of job doesn't make one a different person. At least I hope not."

A Working-class Boy from Lübeck

Grandfather knew the most fascinating stories. His four-year-old grandson sat on his lap and listened. Brandt's earliest memory of his gradfather is of a bearded man who one day dropped in out of the blue in a field-grey uniform. He propped his rifle against the bedroom wall; his tin helmet went on top of the wardrobe. Grandpa had come on leave from the front.

That was in 1917. Hunger was rampant in Germany and the modest worker's flat in Lübeck smelled of turnips. Not that life had been sumptuous there at the best of times. Grandfather and Mother belonged to Lübeck's poor.

In his young days, Grandfather had been a farmhand on a count's estate in Western Mecklenburg. He would tell the little boy indignantly how his own father had been placed over a trestle, hands and feet tied, and beaten.

With that picture always before him, Brandt's grandfather had grown into a rebel. He had come to Lübeck and become a factory lorry driver. He had also become a class-conscious socialist.

He disdained telling his little grandson fairy-tales. The heroes of his stories were Karl Marx, August Bebel and Ferdinand Lassalle. "No God, no King or Emperor will save us—we've got to save ourselves!" the lorry-driver sang to the child on his knee. He would paint passionate pictures of a better future for the workers once they seized their chance. He made it sound a positively idyllic world—socialism sentimental style.

Willy Brandt recalls : "Grandfather also told me that some day there would no longer be any need for money to exist. Everyone would get as much as he was entitled to and at a later stage as much as he needed."

Brandt spent only his earliest years with his mother, whose

name he bore. When *Herbert Ernst Karl Frahm* was born December 18, 1913, the little shopgirl in the grocery store was just nineteen.

The boy's father was never mentioned at home. Brandt says: "I do not know my father and have never wanted to know him. In fact, I never even wondered what qualities I may have inherited from him."

While young Martha Frahm stood behind the grocery counter, a neighbour looked after her little boy. When the First World War was over, Grandfather came home and acted as the child's father. In his wallet Grandpa carried a rather inartistic photograph which Martha had sent him to the front. In it the little boy stands stiffly on a chair, attired in Imperial German uniform and spiked helmet, a wooden rifle cradled in his arm.

Before long, Grandfather remarried. The child now had a step-grandmother, but he never really got to like her. Some years later, his mother married as well. Willy Brandt's stepfather was a builder's foreman. The couple later had a son, but Martha's first-born went on living in his grandfather's household.

Willy Brandt was deeply attached to the simple, decent man. He says of those days: "We lived in a small flat in a newly built block. There were just a couple of rooms and a small bathroom. My room was in the attic. The rent was fifty marks, as much as Grandfather made in a week. He felt he had very much come up in the world, compared with the old days."

Yet once in a while the family knew real hunger. At one time Grandfather was laid off, at another he would be involved in a strike. During one such strike the nine-year-old had an experience that impressed him profoundly. He was pressing his little nose against the baker's window when Grandfather's boss, the director of the Draeger Works, happened to pass by. Noticing the hungry child, he bought two big loaves and placed them in the spindly little arms. The boy dashed home happily, but he was in for a surprise. Grandfather was furious. He addressed the child sharply, saying: "Take those loaves back where they came from, at once. We don't want charity, we want our rights. We aren't taking bribes from the enemy!"

Young Herbert obeyed and realised that "we" meant the poor, the striking workmen, the exploited class. The "enemy" meant the rich, the ruling class, and therefore also the compassionate director outside the baker's.

The growing boy was alone much of the time. At home in the working-class quarter of St Lorenz beyond the Holstentor, as well as at school. Brandt remembers that his was not an easy childhood, but he does not wish to dramatize it or make it sound worse than it was. He says that his grandfather and his mother, whom he used to see once or twice a week, looked after him to the best of their ability. Although at times, he concedes, he would painfully realise the difference between his classmates and himself.

At school young Herbert did very well. He read a lot and was at the top of his form. Like every other boy in Lübeck, he had hopes of going to sea one day. Asked what he was going to be when he grew up, he would answer without hesitating: "I'll be a naval officer."

Under Grandfather's influence, the boy joined the children's group of the working men's sports club. From there he advanced to the Social Democratic *Kinderfreunde* and the Workers' Mandolin Club. Then he joined the 'Red Falcons' and in time rose to membership of the Lübeck branch of the Socialist Youth Union, of which he eventually became chairman.

Years later Willy Brandt said: "As a working-class boy it was easy for me to join the SPD. One might say I was born into it."

At thirteen, the bright and gifted boy got into secondary school— he was exempt from paying school fees. The next year he changed to the *Johanneum*, Lübeck's grammar school, on a scholarship.

There were bound to arise problems; a working-class boy was an exception at the grammar school, and Brandt was being made to feel an outcast. He withdrew from the crowd and became reserved. At recess he would often stand alone in a corner. Proudly, yet also defiantly, he often came to classes wearing the Young Socialists' blue shirt and red tie.

Young Herbert's favourite subjects were German, history and religion. His school leaving certificate of 1932 records *"sehr gut"* or top marks for religion.

But the subject he loved best of all was one that was not being taught in German grammar schools—politics. His headmaster warned his mother: "Keep your son out of politics"—but it was

Willy Brandt

Willy Brandt

too late for that. He had joined the 'Red Falcons' as early as 1928 and soon after become the leader of the 'Karl Marx Group'. The following year, the Lübeck branch of the Young Socialists elected the fifth-form schoolboy local chairman as well as district deputy chairman.

At about that time Herbert's German master picked the most talented boy in class to recite a poem at the *Reichsgründungsfeier,* a highly patriotic affair commemorating the founding of the Second German Empire on January 18, 1871.

The young Socialist could not have been less impressed. About that experience Brandt says : "In protest I put on a bright-red tie, with the result that I was sent home. It was intended as punishment but I was delighted."

Both pupils and masters at the *Johanneum* had nicknamed young Frahm "the politician". When taking matric, he was allowed to do his history essay about August Bebel.

By 1930, Herbert Frahm, though not yet seventeen, was a full-fledged member of the Social Democratic party. Actually, the age limit for membership was eighteen, but a friend had smoothed things out, and an exception was made in his case.

That friend was Julius Leber, a prominent Socialist who represented Lübeck in the *Reichstag.* Leber became the youth's tutor and intercessor.

In those days Herbert Frahm was a lanky youngster with a blond mane who wore plus-fours, coarse kneesocks and a dark blue sailor's cap. Willy Brandt says about that phase of his life : "I was a wild-eyed youth."

It was the year 1932 and he had just passed matric. His childhood dream of becoming a sailor had been forgotten. When asked before leaving school what career he had in mind, he answered, that of a "newspaper writer", for he deemed it unfit for a German to use the foreign term 'journalist'. However, the teaching body had no such qualms, and so his school-leaving certificate records under intended career : journalist.

Encouraged by his German master, the boy had begun to write at fourteen. The *Volksbote,* Lübeck's SPD journal, published young Frahm's reports of local party events. As a matter of fact, he even was awarded a prize for his writing, a leather bound edition of *Leather Stocking* by J.F. Cooper.

11

Thirty years later, when Willy Brandt visited Israel, he had a reunion with the publisher of the Lübeck *Volksbote,* Jakob Gottgetreu. Gottgetreu smiled at the governing mayor of Berlin and said : "I hope my secretariat settled all your fees and I don't owe you any money."

Brandt was able to reassure him on that point. He even remembered that his rate of payment had been five marks per contribution.

In an article circulated a few years ago about his Lübeck days, Gottgetreu wrote about the strikingly handsome fair-haired youth who regularly brought his manuscripts to the editorial office. "He was promising journalistic material," he recalled, "and our chief editor, Dr Leber, thought a great deal of him."

Once, however, the budding writer met with rebuke for an account he wrote about anglers on the Trave river. The Socialist Fishing Club complained to the editor : "Some silly reporter who doesn't know the first thing about angling has made up some story . . ."

Young Frahm prudently decided to stick to politics in future. His first journalistic attempts were aided and promoted by the influential Dr Julius Leber, SPD deputy and chief editor of the *Volksbote.* Born in humble circumstances in the Elsace in 1891, Leber had worked his way through college and risen to the leadership of the Lübeck Social Democrats. To young Herbert Frahm he was more than a mentor in the journalistic trade; Brandt says that Leber was a father figure to him, adding : "His was a decisive influence on my life."

The *Volksbote* also published the schoolboy's first impressions of other countries. In 1928 he had been to Vejle in Denmark under a school exchange scheme; in the summer of 1931 he and a friend travelled to the Scandinavian countries. Frahm especially liked Norway—which was later to become his adopted country—and its "bracing and beautiful" capital, Oslo.

At seventeen, the senior schoolboy took up smoking. Before long, he changed from cigarettes to a pipe to which he stuck for many years. Even now, he will occasionally smoke a pipe but only in private because "the pipe-smoking image is reserved for Herbert Wehner".

12

In the early thirties, many young Socialists rebelled against what they called the "feeble, spineless and compromise-ridden SPD". To be sure, the Social Democrats were sitting on the opposition benches in Berlin, but they "tolerated" the government led by *Zentrum* Chancellor Brüning as the "lesser evil".

Herbert Frahm was one of those impatient, radical youngsters. It was not only political inexperience that made them overshoot the target, nor was it merely disenchantment with their party's impotence. Above all, it was their socialist idealism that impelled the young visionaries to the far left. Issues of dogmatic platforms meant more to them than political realities. Disenchanted with the Weimar State, they just did not care very deeply about it.

Willy Brandt remembers that he and his friends marched in the May Day Parade of 1931, carrying a banner inscribed : *"Republik das ist nicht viel—Sozialismus ist das Ziel"* (The Republic does not mean much—our goal is socialism).

"That evening," he recalls, "my grandfather spoke to me and said angrily : 'How can you be so ungrateful!' I only realized much later what he meant." Meanwhile, discontent was spreading in the ranks of the SPD. Julius Leber too was worried about the party. But he hoped and worked for an opening to the right. It was his opinion that the Socialist party would have to break down the limitations of a pure class party and become a shelter also "for the middle-class youth which had lost its home in the war and is seeking a new fatherland".

Herbert Frahm, however, had different ideas. He was hoping for the revolutionary breakthrough of the working class. By October 1931, the break in the SPD became official. Under the leadership of Max Seydewitz and Kurt Rosenfeld a left radical group split off, founding the Socialist Workers' Party or SAP. Herbert Frahm revelled in his first taste of revolt. He joined the splinter group. One effect of this act was an estrangement between Julius Leber and his protégé. Leber had implored the youngster to refrain from taking that step. Alluding to the chairman of the new party, Seydewitz, he said : "You don't belong to that club of cripples and blind dreamers. Are you out of your mind? Young as you are, you yet know how to appreciate a good book, a fine wine and a pretty girl. In short, you're perfectly normal and don't belong to those sectarians."

But the young man was not to be swayed. At a Trade Union House meeting in the old *Johannisgasse* he was the only one who dared to oppose and contradict Leber in the discussion, firmly convinced of the virtue of his arguments.

His leap to the left and his dispute with Leber marked the end of Herbert's writing for the *Volksbote*. Having passed matric, he wished to enrol at the university. But he needed money and meanwhile joined a firm of ship brokers as a clerk. Even now Brandt recalls : "I was paid thirty marks a month, my first regular income."

At the same time he was busy learning foreign languages. Not only out of books and in the office but also during many long talks on the Lübeck dockside with foreign seamen. His evenings were reserved for politics. There were ever fiercer clashes with the National Socialists, streetfighting and beerhall battles with the Storm Troopers. It was a last desperate attempt to stem the tide. But disaster was approaching fast. January 30, 1933 brought the takeover of the Nazis, celebrated with torch parades and triumphal marches but also with persecution and terror unleashed at the opponents of the regime.

On February 1, Julius Leber was arrested. Storm Troopers had attacked the SPD deputy on his way home and beaten him up. Leber was taken to prison with severe injuries.

The ranks of both SPD and SAP were outraged. Towards the end of their last futile stand against the Nazis, Herbert Frahm had made up his political quarrel with Leber. Being the chairman of the Lübeck SAP branch, he now became the youngest member of a delegation sent to the local trade union leader to call for a general strike in protest of Leber's arrest and mistreatment. Yet the worthy union functionary dismissed them with astonishment and disapproval : "Don't you know that strikes are illegal now?"

In the following years Leber became one of the heroes of the resistance struggle against Hitler. With short intervals he was held in various prisons and concentration camps until 1937. Then he was released and went to Berlin to become a coal merchant, both to earn his living and to establish contact with the underground movement. Later on Leber played a major role in the attempt on Hitler's life of July 20, 1944, and was sentenced to death by

Willy Brandt at the Conference Table

Willy Brandt and Herbert Wehner

Willy Brandt and Helmut Schmidt

the People's Court. Leber was executed in Plötzensee on January 5, 1945.

Before his death he wrote to friends from prison : "For a cause so fine and just one's life is but a fair price to pay."

After the Nazi takeover, the left-wing SAP, which had gained a substantial following in Saxony and Silesia, was outlawed as well. For a while the clandestine national party leadership tried to continue its activities. It called a secret national conference to be held in Dresden on March 12, 1933. The young Lübeck party chairman went there via Berlin, his first visit to the German capital.

He travelled in disguise. "My less than subtle costume," he remembers, "was a brightly coloured cloth cap."

But he also adopted a more important disguise : "After discussing the matter with my closest friends, I first called myself *Willy Brandt*."

Although it had been intended as a temporary device, he never again discarded the new name. Herbert Ernst Karl Frahm was a thing of the past. The nineteen-year-old entered a new chapter of his life.

Willy Brandt in Private

Willy Brandt is just a fraction under six feet tall. He weighs a little over 13 and a half stone, once a year temporarily gets his slight overweight down to 12 and a half, "with a lot of trouble", by taking spa treatment, as a rule at Bad Kreuth.

He has hazel eyes and pepper-and-salt hair. Of the characteristic tuft of hair above his forehead, Rut Brandt says : "It has the same relationship to the rest of his hair as Berlin has to the Federal Republic."

The former deputy protocol chief in Bonn, Frau Erica Pappritz, ranks Brandt among "the best-dressed German political figures". In 1967, the German tie institute voted him "tie wearer of the year". In private, Brandt is fond of easy, casual clothes. He wears sports shirts, hand-knitted jerseys and cardigans, Bavarian style shooting jackets.

The Chancellor is a great reader. He reads in bed, on free weekends and on holiday. His favourite subjects are history and politics, biographies, technical books and semi-documentary novels. In order to get through the heaps of reading matter placed before him by his staff and friends, Brandt uses a speed-reading method, letting his eyes travel diagonally across the page.

Among his hobbies are watching TV, fishing, hiking and walking, swimming and, less often, skiing. At one time he used to collect coins.

Brandt calls his musical tastes "catholic". His favourite composers are Beethoven, Bach and Grieg. But he adds : "In recent years I have found to my own surprise that I also like modern composers. I have listened to some of their works and think I understand them."

In his days as Foreign Minister, Brandt had more social obligations than nowadays. If there are dinner guests at his house,

they are likely to be government—and party friends. He confesses :
"Old ties of friendship are stronger than new. When I meet people
from the old days, I try to find more time for them than I can
spare for new friends."

Willy Brandt is fond of telling political jokes. His favourite
subject of conversation, even at home, is politics. Rut Brandt
has said in mock despair : "I sometimes think he even dreams
politics."

Asked about his favourite dishes, the Chancellor lists smoked
meat and spring cabbage, a Norwegian dish called Farikal (stewed
lamb and cabbage), boiled beef and horse-radish sauce, lentil soup,
potato pancakes and lobster. He stopped taking hard drink some
years ago. Nowadays he drinks Moselle wine, Campari and soda,
port, or Coca-Cola with a dash of brandy; if very thirsty, beer.
He has also changed his smoking habits, from the cigarettes he
used to chainsmoke to cigarillos. Occasionally, he will cadge a
cigarette from a companion. "The ones you cadge taste best,"
he says with a grin.

Is Willy Brandt thin-skinned? Is he easily hurt? The man who
has had to put up with many a mud-slinging campaign over the
years says simply : "It is hard to judge oneself. Anyway, I'm no
rhinoceros."

Brandt's Life and Work
for Two Countries

The night of March 31, 1933 was a dark and stormy one. As Paul Stooss, a Travemünde fisherman, sailed his small trawler through the rough Baltic sea, a young man in a trench-coat was crouching in a corner of the deck, hidden behind some crates and barrels. Willy Brandt was travelling to freedom with 100 marks in his pocket. A couple of clean shirts and the first volume of Marx's *Das Kapital* were in his briefcase. Years later Brandt commented : "*Das Kapital* did not manage to turn me into a dyed-in-the-wool marxist."

After the five-hour crossing, Brandt stepped ashore at Rödbyhavn on the Danish island of Lolland. He spent the next few days in Copenhagen in the flat of the worker poet Oscar Hansen, then went on to Norway. In Oslo he was being expected.

Just turned nineteen, he had left behind him name, family and homeland. His flight had been a necessity because his name was on the Nazis' black list and his arrest a matter of days. Moreover, his party, the SAP, had delegated him to build up a system of foreign contacts in Norway. The new Oslo party office was charged with revealing the true state of affairs in Germany to the Scandinavian public, and with marshalling both material and moral support for the fight against Hitler's regime.

Among the party friends Brandt left behind in Lübeck was a girl called Gertrud. The letters he sent her from Oslo had resistance slogans written between the lines in invisible ink; they almost sealed her fate. One day she was summoned to local Nazi headquarters and at the last moment remembered the letter in her handbag. Wasting no time, she chewed up and swallowed the paper and managed to go home unscathed.

Willy Brandt came to Norway on a political mission. But he

was also determined to be different from the run-of-the-mill emigrés. "I neither could nor would look back all the time," he said. "I tried to sink roots as fast as I could and not to remain an outcast."

The first few years were hard. "I did not indulge in riotous living as some would like to pretend," he said in 1960 at the height of the smearing campaign against him. "But when you are young you don't mind dry bread for breakfast and an 80 Öre lunch at the feeding centre."

Brandt plunged into work. He managed the Oslo SAP bureau and was chairman of the local refugee organisation. He read philosophy and modern history at Oslo University and quickly established friendly relations with a number of leading leftwing personalities on the Scandinavian political scene. He also found time to work in the Norwegian youth movement, where all-night discussions about the aims of socialism were frequent occurrences. In addition, he worked for the educational branch of the Norwegian Workers' Party and was secretary of the Norwegian public relief scheme.

After a few months or so, Brandt spoke Norwegian well. He had been able to read it when he arrived and gained fluency in no time at all. Brandt says : "Before long I spoke Norwegian as easily as my mother tongue."

The Socialist resistance groups inside Germany supplied Brandt's Oslo bureau with illegal newspapers and leaflets; Brandt wrote articles—mainly for the press service of the socialists dailies and the trade union press—and gave lectures about the true situation in Hitler's Germany. He maintained ties with various groups of German exiles all over Europe and travelled extensively, to Denmark, England, Holland, France and Czechoslovakia.

Yet his most daring trip was to Berlin. During the second half of 1936 Brandt spent several months in the German capital, gaining more first-hand experience of life in the 'Third Reich'. French friends had selected him as political head of the organisation *Metro,* set up to coordinate and exchange experience of underground work with Berlin resistance groups.

Carrying a passport in the name of Gunnar Gassland, Norwegian student, Willy Brandt rented a furnished room from a Frau Hamel at 20 *Kurfürstendamm*. Berlin was teeming with foreigners and gay with flags, for 1936 was the year of the Olympic Games; and the bustle aided Brandt in the execution of his dangerous work. He later wrote : "I met with instances of splendid loyalty and found some Berliners sincerely ready to help; there were those with that 'long tongue but good heart' characteristic of the people of Berlin who would not succumb even to Nazi pressure."

In February 1937 Willy Brandt went to Spain, where the Civil War was raging. As a correspondent for Scandinavian papers he reported from the battlefronts. He also established contacts in Barcelona for the SAP. He had taken Spanish in grammar school (his fourth foreign language), and now the knowledge came in handy.

The young left-wing socialist naturally supported the Republications. But the constant bickering and intrigue in their ranks, as well as the Soviet Union's massive intervention—not so unlike the actions of Fascist Italy and Nazi Germany—made Willy Brandt leave Spain a very thoughtful young man.

His Civil War experiences and the lessons he learned from them earned him rebuke from opposing sides in later years. The communists described him as a 'social fascist' and 'Gestapo spy', whereas his right-wing adversaries called him a 'Red'.

Back in Oslo, Brandt met Carlota, a young Norwegian secretary at the Institute for Comparative Cultural Research. In 1940 the two set up a simple home together. However, Hitler's armies invaded Norway, and Willy and Carlota had to delay their marriage which later took place in Stockholm.

Norway was invaded on April 9, 1940. Brandt was wanted by the Gestapo. His German citizenship had been abrogated as early as 1938, and though he had applied for Norwegian citizenship, his case was still being investigated. Stateless, he was in grave danger.

Norwegian friends of his came to the rescue. Within hours of the invasion, they were taking Brandt by car to Mittetdalen on Norway's west coast. There they got him a Norwegian uniform. The trick worked. After a few weeks of internment as a 'prinsoner of war' Brandt was released by the Germans to go "home to my native city Oslo".

That episode was to earn Brandt much vilification in later years.

His opponents made the most of it, asserting that he had joined the Norwegian army and 'shot at his German countrymen'. Brandt's slanderers kept up their campaign until he put a stop to it by having the truth established in a German court.

With Norway occupied, Brandt saw no way of continuing his work there. So he escaped to Sweden with the help of a friend. The document granting him Norwegian citizenship was forwarded to Stockholm by the exiled Norwegian government in London. For the duration of the war, Brandt had become a dual emigré, a German refugee to Norway and a Norwegian national who had fled to Stockholm.

In Sweden he carried on his political and journalistic work. He became chief editor of the Swedish-Norwegian Press Agency, wrote books and worked in the refugee organisation. Several months after his flight, Carlota also arrived in Stockholm with their new-born baby girl, Ninja. The couple married but separated shortly before the end of the war. Brandt met his second wife—a Norwegian like his first—in the press section of the Norwegian Embassy in Stockholm and married her in Berlin after the war. Their three sons were all born in the German capital.

From Sweden Willy Brandt wrote to a friend:

"I have twice lost my country. Now I am working to regain two homelands, a free Norway and a democratic Germany."

In 1945, after the collapse of Hitler's *Reich,* Brandt went back to Norway, where, as he once said, he "spent years which in many respects were the most important of my life" and where he "gained important and indispensable experience and understanding". Norway, his adopted homeland, "marked me indelibly for the rest of my life"

The Woman by Brandt's Side

Norwegian-born Rut Brandt is, as she puts it, "a trained German". Early in 1967 after the formation of the 'Grand Coalition', she followed her husband to Bonn, but did so with reservations, for she was reluctant to part from Berlin, where she had lived by her husband's side through the city's proud and fateful hours. Her three sons had been born there, indeed, Berlin had come to be like home.

But Bonn welcomed Rut Brandt with open arms and by now she is quite used to living there.

When Rut Hansen from Hamar in Norway met her future husband in Stockholm in 1944, they were both refugees. She had fled to Sweden when her resistance group was uncovered. In Stockholm she worked in the press section of the Norwegian Embassy, while Brandt managed the Swedish-Norwegian Press Agency. At the end of the war, after a short visit to Norway, Brandt returned to Germany as press attaché of the Norwegian Military Mission in Berlin. Rut followed a few months later. In 1948 they were married "despite the adverse conditions and our uncertain future" (Brandt). For both of them it was their second marriage. In Stockholm Rut had married a childhood friend, the railwayman Bergaust who had died of TB late in 1946. Willy Brandt's first marriage ended in divorce at the end of the war. The road the couple now walked together took them through every chapter of the dramatic story of postwar Berlin. Eventually Brandt gave up his post as a Norwegian diplomat. He joined the Social Democratic Party and once more plunged into politics.

With her charm, wisdom and understanding, Rut Brandt has contributed a great deal to her husband's career.

She knows how to move in public with self-assurance, tact

Even on Holiday—At Work with
Federal Minister Horst Ehmke

Willy Brandt with Federal Economic
Minister Karl Schiller

Willy Brandt at a Campaign Conference

Willy Brandt with Conrad Ahlers,
Head of the Federal Press Department

and subtlety. In her prominent position, she retains her unaffected, pleasant ways. "That tangy, unpretentious Scandinavian simplicity is what lends this attractive woman her special charm" is how one of her many admirers, Bonn's 'Court Chronicler' Walter Henkels, describes the Chancellor's wife.

In the *Venusberg* residence Rut is a perfect hostess. Her sons declare that she is a wonderful mother as well. Brandt himself regrets that politics leaves him little time to spend with his family: "It's a pity that I cannot devote myself more to my wife and sons," he says.

He has never ceased to be grateful to his wife for giving up her journalistic career earlier, because her marriage, family and home came first. Although Willy Brandt is known as the most unflappable of men, he contends that he is too nervous to drive. In consequence, Rut Brandt also acts as family chauffeur.

What Rut has meant to Willy Brandt along his long and turbulent road from Scandinavia to Berlin and on to Bonn is best expressed in his own words: "My best friend is my wife."

Berlin, a Very Special City

It is difficult to think of anything in history as absurd or arbitrary as the divided state and isolation of the former German capital which had been Germany's capital for 74 years. One half free, the other in bondage, yet both inseparably linked. The city's fate was determined by the Allies at the conference table, and their irrevocable decision was carried out down to the last detail.

What was left of Berlin when the guns of the Second World War had fallen silent was no city but a bled-dry, gutted torso which could hardly be revived. Perhaps it should have been cleared, as Carthage was after the Punic Wars. For the time being, and probably for decades to come, the late capital could scarcely be of any importance even if it were rebuilt as a mass settlement amidst the great sandy plain.

In the early postwar years Berlin, destroyed by the ravages of war, looked a dead city. In the cruel winters that followed hundreds of old and sick people and infants froze to death in their beds for there was nothing to warm them. Even the last chair in the house and the last tree in the *Tiergarten* had been used for firewood.

It was to this Berlin that Willy Brandt came as press attaché of the Norwegian Military Mission, wearing the uniform of a Norwegian major. His rank, however, was a mere formality, for an oval badge on his sleeve identified him as a 'Civilian Officer'. His friend, Norwegian Foreign Minister Halvard Lange, had offered him a diplomatic post in Paris, but Brandt had unhesitatingly rejected it in favour of Berlin.

By the end of 1946, Brandt knew the whole harsh, ubiquitous reality of the bomb-destroyed and crushed country. His first visit had taken him to Lübeck, his old home town. There was no rejoicing about that homecoming, even though both his mother and half-brother were alive and well.

Willy Brandt heard no reproaches for having been abroad. Neither in Lübeck nor in Nürnberg, where he went to cover the war crimes trials for Norwegian papers. And not in Frankfurt either, where in February 1946 he first faced the symbol of the shattered Germany, Dr Kurt Schumacher, the potential representative of a new national consciousness. A dynamo of will power, Schumacher was yet marked by death. He had lost his right arm in the First World War; later his left leg had been amputated, indeed his whole organism was poisoned by the years of suffering in the concetration camp. Schumacher was actually dying by inches.

His office, the 'Büro Dr Schumacher', fundamentally followed the left-orientated line, yet not in the sense of the Communist International. Grotewohl and his Berlin cohorts favoured capitulation to the communist demand for a forced merger of the two Socialist parties, SPD and KPD, which was eventually implemented to form the East German SED *(Sozialistische Einheitspartei Deutschlands)*. Schumacher waged the first political battle for the future of the still undivided city of Berlin, and won.

Willy Brandt owed his first contact with Berlin to a friend of Leber's, Gustav Dahrendorf. In those days Brandt did a lot of travelling. In Bielefeld, at the first trade union congress, he met Max Brauer, the future mayor of Hamburg who had returned to Germany from the U.S.A.; in Lübeck Brandt made his first public speech, and in Travemünde he privately called on the fisherman who had taken him to Denmark thirteen years before.

At about the same time as Brandt, another expatriate arrived in the German capital. It was Ernst Reuter, back from Turkey, where he had spent the Nazi years as a professor in Ankara. Reuter later became mayor to guide the destiny of free Berlin. If Julius Leber had been Willy Brandt's first mentor, Reuter became his second.

In May, 1946, SPD leaders called the first party conference in Hanover. From the 'East', only the Berlin delegates attended. The second party conference was held in Nürnberg in June 1947. At that time the office of Berlin's acting mayor was in the hands of Louise Schröder, a Social Democrat. In the first postwar election her party had won the largest number of seats—63 out of 130—in Berlin's city parliament.

A tough and unbending opponent was Communist Party chief Wilhelm Pieck. He struck Willy Brandt, who had called on him as press attaché, as something of a communist Hindenburg. Kurt Schumacher counselled Brandt to take over the *Verbindungsetelle* (public relations department) of the Berlin Party Presidium, also to apply for reinstatement as a German national. Brandt followed his advice on both counts. When he took up that office on January 1, 1948, he was only 34. Four months later the provincial government in Kiel renewed his German citizenship with a proviso confirming Willy Brandt as his official name.

It was the time when the people of Berlin had to undergo their hardest endurance test since the war. George Marshall had announced the generous U.S. plan for the rebuilding of Europe that bore his name; the Truman Doctrine had saved Greece from a communist takeover. Stalin was looking for new pastures and sought to find them in the West, inside Germany.

On March 18, 1948, Ernst Reuter, addressing 80,000 Berliners outside the destroyed *Reichstag* building, said : "Prague has gone, Finland was meant to go. Whose turn is it next? It will not be Berlin's. The communist flood shall break against our iron will." West Berlin was being punished but did not capitulate. In time the big airlift was perfected to the point when a plane landed in the city every 63 seconds. The Allies were bringing in nearly twice as much as the minimum need of 4500 tons of supplies. When the Russians finally lifted the blockade after 322 days—on May 12, 1949—39 Britons, 31 Americans and 9 Germans had lost their lives in the Allied airlift for the freedom of Berlin.

When the first national elections of 1949 drew near, Schumacher offered his Berlin delegate a safe constituency in Schleswig-Holstein. However, Brandt declined; he was sent to the first *Bundestag* as the Berlin municipal parliament's delegate. That first Bonn *Bundestag* was marked by the intellectual contrast between the Rhinelander Adenauer and the West-Prussian Schumacher. It came under sharp attack from Ernst Reuter who said : "If I were Chancellor, I'd go to Berlin and set up the Federal government there. The Russians won't go to war over that." At a later time he said : "The biggest political mistake of these years was to move the provisionary capital to the left bank of the Rhine."

In August 1952 occurred the death of Kurt Schumacher, the greatest socialist of the postwar era. One parliamentary term had been enough for him to refurbish his party's political image and to steer the Social Democrats on a path that was some day bound to lead to the government benches. Politicians of all parties were getting set for a new election campaign, when on June 17, 1953 Berlin became the centre of resistance against the communist regime. The draconian measures used to put down the popular rising were doubtless instrumental in making many West Germans give their votes to the Christian Democrats. Adenauer's party polled five million votes. Strengthened by that massive mandate, the Chancellor was able to pursue with even greater vigour his "no experiments" policy, as the CDU election slogan had pledged.

On October 1, 1953, Willy Brandt made his first big speech in Berlin. Ernst Reuter had died two days previously. In tribute to the city's mayor, the crowd of mourning Berliners heard Brandt say : "You were our teacher, our exhorter and our good friend."

In the second German *Bundestag,* Brandt was elected to the presidium of the SPD Fraction; however, party comrades were not quite ready to see him fly so high. He was defeated at the two party congresses of 1954 and 1956. Finally he made it at the third, in Stuttgart in 1958.

By now, the Berliners were accustomed to their city's permanent state of siege and the continuous whine of Soviet jet fighters over-head; they had also got used to the endless military parades and rallies in the Eastern sector. But when in November 1956 the Hungarian people rose in their heroic but doomed fight against oppression and were desperately waiting for a sign from the free West, a wave of sympathy and support surged through West Berlin. To Willy Brandt, delegate and Deputy Provincial Chairman of the SPD, it was a supreme opportunity to show his mettle. The throng outside the Schöneberg townhall kept calling for action; and Brandt directed the excited crowd to march to *Steinplatz* in order to keep it away from the Eastern sector. The people followed Brandt's appeal, yet feelings were running dangerously high. On June 17th Street he had to calm his marchers down over

27

the public address system of a police car. The chief target of the Berliners' displeasure were the police blocking the way of some thousands of young Germans who wished to march through the Brandenburg Gate to express their indignation at the Soviet Embassy in East Berlin. Just a couple of hundred yards away from the ranks of *Volkspolizei* lined up beyond the Brandenburg Gate, machine-guns ready to fire, Brandt finally managed to turn back the crowd.

At that time the governing mayor of Berlin, Professor Otto Suhr, fell seriously ill. In the search for a possible successor, Brandt's name first cropped up in 1956. He had meanwhile risen to chairman of the Berlin Assembly.

When Suhr died the following year, Brandt was almost unanimously nominated by his party and won the post with a large majority. As he accepted the congratulations, he wore a grin, but he turned serious the next instant. "I have taken on a heavy burden," he said.

How heavy a burden became obvious very soon, for Brandt's enemies began to harrass him, not even shying away from spreading fabrications about the governing mayor's past. And yet, the slander meant little compared to the campaign that was unleashed when Brandt later attempted to represent his party in the Federal Republic proper.

Meanwhile, however, Berlin had to be rebuilt. While early efforts had lacked in purpose and co-ordination, the job was now being tackled vigorously and systematically. The new town was planned on a generous scale and its construction received massive help and support from West Germany. By the time Willy Brandt handed his office over to his successor, West Berlin had grown into Germany's biggest industrial city.

12 Kiefernweg, Venusberg, Bonn

The house stands in parklike grounds, with big, old trees lining the spacious lawn. The Foreign Minister's official residence on Bonn's Venusberg ranks among the finest in the Federal capital. When Foreign Minister Brandt became Chancellor, he showed no desire to move out of the house and into the Chancellor's Bungalow in the park of Palais Schaumburg. And as the new Foreign Minister, Walter Scheel, who had just moved into a new house, also on Venusberg, was not interested in a move either, they both kept their addresses and saved the Bonn housing authorities a lot of headaches.

Originally built by an industrialist, 12 Kiefernweg became the residence of SPD Chairman Kurt Schumacher. In the mid-fifties it was purchased by the administration as the Foreign Minister's official residence. Succeeding Foreign Ministers von Brentano and Schröder, Brandt moved in early in 1967.

The groundfloor of the eleven-room house is entered by a glassed-in porch. It is reserved for official purposes. On a small hall table lies the finely-bound guest book.

The main downstairs room is a large drawing-room with upholstered suites and mahogany butler tables. On oriental rugs stand standard lamps with silver—and porcelain stands. The length wall is decorated with a big Brussels tapestry depicting Carthage's surrender to Scipio. Along the shorter walls stand glass cases and cabinets. All the furnishings are government property. "What belongs to us," says Rut Brandt, "are the things in the cupboards and on the tables." Those things are souvenirs and presents brought back from trips abroad, like a Japanese doll, a wooden bull from Venezuela, East-Asian silverware, small Roman amphorae and old china.

To the right of the drawing-room is the bay-windowed smoking room. It too is furnished with comfortable armchairs and settees. There is a large desk with a bust of President Kennedy on a black marble stand.

The big corner room to the left of the drawing-room is the dining-room seating up to thirty dinner guests. Behind it lie the kitchen quarters.

Wide glass doors at the back of the house lead to an awning-covered terrace and beyond to a small heated swimming pool. The reception rooms and the garden are looked after by the care-taker couple, Herr and Frau Weber.

Upstairs is the Brandts' private flat; sitting-room and dining-room, study, bedrooms and kitchen. Frau Brandt has a maid to help with the housework. In the Chancellor's bedroom stands a desk made from old shipping crates. One wall is taken up by floor-to-ceiling book-cases, in front of them is a librarian's ladder, a present to Brandt from his wife.

Rut Brandt has furnished her bright and cosy room, a semi-circular one overlooking the garden, with brightly covered arm-chairs, an old English bureau and white book-cases.

Matthias, the family 'baby', points out proudly that one whole wall in his room is his own to draw and paint on. His room is on the same floor as his parents', while his older brother, Lars, is comfortably settled on the top floor which is reached by a narrow staircase. The oldest son, Peter, lives and studies in Berlin.

Finally, the Chancellor's household is completed by a Hungarian sheepdog called *Huszar,* a Siamese cat answering to *Nusse,* a golden hamster and—if it has not run away again—a tortoise.

Brandt Campaigning

As early as the summer of 1961 John Gunther wrote: "There may soon be a political changeover in the Federal Republic of Germany. Willy Brandt, the 47 year-old governing mayor of Berlin and the Socialists' candidate for the chancellorship, is a dangerous opponent to the ruling party.

"With less than three months to go till the fourth national election, the most fundamental features of the Socialist 'class party' have faded and given way to the image of an emerging 'people's party'. With 32 per cent of the vote in the 1957 election, the SPD has gained a platform from which it would like to take off for the leap into the government.

"At present, though, this seems to be an undertaking wrought with difficulty. Konrad Adenauer continues to be the crucial man in German postwar politics. There may be many a German currently guided by the maxim: 'I really don't like Adenauer, but I can't imagine things going on without him'.

"Against this old politican—who can at times be maddeningly stubborn but is perhaps the more successful for it—any attempt at opposition appears futile."

By then, Brandt had been governing mayor of Berlin for four years, since October 3, 1957. Being pushed into the frontline of the free world by virtue of his office, he had grown into one of the most notable personalities of his party whose moderate wing he presented. At that time much was being made of the question of whether clinging to tradition mattered more than adapting to changed outlooks. But Brandt was more concerned about power than about party doctrine. He made it perfectly clear that interparty polemics would have to wait until the SPD held the power.

To foreign observers at that stage Brandt was perhaps the most attractive of the leading German Socialists. John Gunther described him as "all warmth, integrity, vigour and self-assurance". He answered questions frankly and with ready wit; he was articulate and indeed in full command of the journalist's tools of trade.

"He has the captivating force of a man radiating personality and a natural, boyish charm."

Brandt's campaign managers had planned to build up the image of "smiling Willy", a faithful European copy of the successful John F. Kennedy. They contrasted the rugged boyishness of the new Socialist Chancellor candidate with grim-visaged, knotty Konrad Adenauer. Yet when the election came, millions of German women, on whose admiration for the elegant and virile man in his prime one had counted, turned overwhelmingly to the grand old man whom Bonn-based newspapermen had nicknamed "John Foster Adenauer" because of the consuming distaste for the "Soffyetts" he shared with the U.S. statesman.

That summer Willy Brandt rushed across the West German provinces at 'seventy miles per hour', making some twenty to thirty speeches a day, from five to thirty minutes each, depending on the size of the town.

Then came the day when the teleprinters started ticking out the message that Walter Ulbricht was about to build a wall. Once more Berlin became the prime focus of the political scene. It was an issue before which the election campaign receded into the background. Brandt declared that henceforth he would be able to spare just one day a week for electioneering. "The election fight is off," he said. "There is just the fight for Berlin ... Why don't we appeal to the United Nations? Why do we keep talking around this problem which the world will have to deal with, this problem which is burning on the world's skin? What has been done to avert this crisis? Nothing! And what is being done now? Again nothing!"

After August 13, Brandt had immediately written to President Kennedy and requested that something be done for Berlin. The Christian Democrats censured him severely, calling his letter an act of arrogance on the part of the governing mayor of Berlin who had dared to go straight to the President over the heads of the West German government.

In the end, the fight for Berlin gained Brandt the Freedom Prize of the American Freedom House Foundation, but not the leap into government. In the election of September 17, 1961, the Social Democrats polled 11.5 million votes—a respectable figure, but not nearly enough to topple the entrenched CDU/CSU.

Disappointment soon gave way to a well-founded optimism. The Socialists had improved their position, from 31.8 to 36.3 per cent of the votes. The number of their direct mandates had risen, and two million new votes had been won. Why not look forward with confidence to the coming year's regional elections? Why not fix one's sights on the next national election to be held in 1965?

Willy Brandt remained his party's top personality, even though he left the leadership of the opposition to veteran politician Erich Ollenhauer.

The Socialists were working hard. In 1961 neither Brandt nor anyone else at party headquarters had seriously believed that the Union of Christian Democrats could be beaten. For 1965, however, the chances were judged to be very real. Consequently, the Social Democrats directed all their efforts at continuing along the way begun with the Godesberg Programme of 1959. The SPD Watchword for the Party Conference in Köln-Deutz that year was 'After our election successes, let us move on'.

Quite early in the struggle, the Socialists had recognized the importance of public relations, whereas the Union parties were lagging behind in that field.

Prospects for 1965 looked fair and Erich Ollenhauer said: "Our position in the *Bundestag* is excellent vis-a-vis any possible attempt to thwart the democratic order in this country by amending the Constitution."

Modern communication strategy does eventually bear fruits: "We should look upon public relations as a lasting need."

As to the next election, Willy Brandt declared: "Today it is clear that we can win a national election. That knowledge has given our friends new self-confidence."

Three and a half years have gone by—it is election night in September 1965.

Asked by newspapermen whether he will return to Berlin or

go on fighting for Bonn, an exhausted Willy Brandt dismisses them with a tired wave of the hand : "Let's talk about that when we've had a good night's sleep."

At 2 a.m., the SPD tiger in the tank of his black Mercedes, whom friends had already imagined driving down Bonn's Koblenz Street, is tired out and seems to be at the end of his strength which he has ruthlessly overtaxed during the six hectic weeks of electioneering.

Little wonder that his only thought is of a good night's sleep. But the newspapermen want his comment, they insist, they demand an analysis of the Socialist's defeat. Willy Brandt is unable to oblige, so is Herbert Wehner who just manages to mumble some grimly humorous remarks out of that corner of his mouth which is not taken up by his pipe.

Election nights may be dull fare to many, to the politicians they are as full of suspense as the moments before the jury files back into court. The world does not come to an end on election night, but it may decide the future of an individual and indeed the fate of a nation.

What pressed heavily on Brandt's mind that night were his many friends all over Germany whose hopes had been dashed. The millions of new votes gained meant little to them; all they could see was that victory had once more eluded them. The goal that seemed to draw closer with each election was still out of reach. As elsewhere in the world, the uninitiated voter in Germany considers anything short of victory an absolute defeat.

The West German parliament is elected for a term of four years. The last months of that period and the steadily rising pitch of the battle for the votes makes the man in the street regard that time as the decisive phase of the contest. The flood of speeches, the endless stream of propaganda and the unceasing mass media coverage certainly make it look as though an election campaign was a period of weeks of political boom.

For the contestants, however, the campaign starts years before, from the time when the majority party prepares to present to the President its list of names for the intended next cabinet.

On the strength of his party's showing in 1961, Willy Brandt's chances as Chancellor candidate had been fair enough for him

Willy Brandt and Klaus Schütz,
Governing Mayor of Berlin

Willy Brandt Signing Autographs
on Hans-Jürgen Wischnewski's back

Willy Brandt Campaigning

Willy Brandt Reading the New York
Times Magazine

to see no need for blandishment or tricks in 1965. Chancellor Erhard was no Adenauer.

The old man had been a wily politician who was not to be out-bluffed. Indeed, he had a knack for making capital out of his opponents' successes. The most exciting event of the election year 1961—the building of the Berlin Wall and the completion of the string of obstacles along the border, turning the strip from Lübeck in the north to Hof in the Bavarian south into a deadly no-man's-land—had gained more votes for Adenauer than it had for Brandt. Yet it was Brandt who had ventured within stone-throw of the Volksarmists of East Berlin, it was he who had turned back the excited throng of West Berliners and personally kept them from rushing into the ready machine guns of the Russians and the People's Army.

As 1965 opened, Willy Brandt was getting ready for the leap to Bonn. The newspapers left no doubt that the election fight was already in full swing. Since the spring of 1964 Brandt had been his party's chairman, succeeding Ollenhauer who had died in December 1963. In Fritz Erler—chairman of the SPD fraction in the *Bundestag* and Vice Chairman of the German Council of the United Europe Movement—the party had its most distinguished politician. Erler's early death was a great blow, for like Kurt Schumacher, Ernst Reuter and Erich Ollenhauer, he had ranked among the party's most brilliant minds.

Other names in Brandt's shadow cabinet were Herbert Wehner, deputy chairman; Dr Karl Schiller, Economics Professor in Hamburg and Economic Senator in Berlin; Dr Alex Möller, Käte Strobel, Professor Carlo Schmid, Vice President of the *Bundestag;* Helmut Schmidt, Senator in the Hamburg parliament; ex-Federal Minister Dr Gustav Heinemann; Waldemar von Knoeringen, Munich deputy; and Professor Ernst Schellenberg.

Most of them were to hold office in the first Socialist government four years later, after having held posts in the Grand Coalition.

Those ten men—counting Brandt—and one woman, who were introduced to the electorate, did not only form Brandt's shadow cabinet; but they were also entrusted with a mandate. Brandt explained it by saying: "We want close relations and steady consultations with the big organisations representing important groups and interests of the population."

Within his party, however, it was felt that Brandt still lacked the image that German TV watchers expected of a prominent leader. Major TV requirements, as everyone knows, are a fluent speaking manner and an air of authority, urbanity and sophistication.

As governing mayor Brandt had established good relations with the public through the local press, yet he had not properly 'arrived' on German TV screens. However, that was a problem that could be dealt with when the time came, for first of all, there were the critics in Brandt's own ranks who had to be appeased.

That job was tackled by Helmut Schmidt at an extraordinary regional conference of Hamburg Social Democrats. Schmidt defended Brandt with vigour, adding that given the chance, he would definitely vote for Brandt as Chancellor. "Willy may not be the glibbest TV talker," said Schmidt, "but he is the best man in a difficult situation."

Much, if not everything, depended on the party chairman. If he and his associates would be able to mobilise many and as yet unknown forces it should be possible to restore sparkle to the images of both party and party chairman and eventually make the popular leader of Berlin the possible leader of the Republic.

It was the time when Brandt was once more in the limelight for the talks he was conducting with East German leaders about the granting of border passes to West Berliners wishing to visit relatives across the Wall in East Berlin. However, on that issue the Christian Democrats held their fire, as its significance was largely local. In consequence, Brandt could not make much political capital out of it with the West German voters. Indeed, as long as he stuck to the Berlin scene, the CDU/CSU saw no reason for any attacks on his person. Yet when it became obvious that he had set his sights on Bonn and was getting active in the pre-election campaign, the government parties sought to eliminate the foe before he entered the arena. Politicians from the parties in power willingly conceded that Brandt might be the right man for Berlin, but did he have the qualities to lead the government?

All of a sudden, everything appeared to go against Brandt. Once more his past was being gone through with a fine comb, as Lothar Brenner, a journalist, was being charged with libel against Brandt in a West Berlin court. The defendant could think of nothing better than to cite Rut Brandt as a witness that Brandt had allegedly fought against German soldiers in the war. An interview with Frau Brandt had appeared in the Danish women's journal, *Alt for Damerne*, quoting her as having said: "Willy fought with the Norwegian troops against the German occupation forces."

On the stand, Rut testified that she had not even discussed that point during the interview. The journal's editors must have inserted the controversial sentence on their own initiative. Frau Brandt was able to prove that in answer to her complaint, the magazine's publishers had apologized to her for that unscrupulous addition.

When young Peter Brandt, who was sixteen at the time, gave vent to his feelings about the United States' military intervention in Vietnam at a youth club conference, that incident also was exploited to question his father's aptitude as a leader. The witch-hunt reached another high point later, when sons Peter and Lars visited a film studio and alarmed a number of journalists by playing a game involving German Second World War medals.

There is little doubt that such incidents would have been less copiously reported if Willy Brandt had quietly and unambitiously stayed on in Berlin. As it was, he had to put up with all sorts of obstacles strewn in his path by political opponents and neutrals alike.

In those days a sensitive observer would have noted that all was not well with West Germany. Behind the facade of prosperity, one could hear a rustle in the woodwork, if one listened closely. Was Chancellor Erhard's widely quoted slogan '*Mass halten*' (observe moderation), that godsent to humorists throughout the country, really enough to keep the people loyal to the Christian Union parties?

Never before had Germany's intellectuals been so active in an election campaign as they were in 1965—a development that should perhaps be investigated by the specialists some day. Apprehension lest the government-held course of smug contentment bring about a uniformity of thinking, a soporific state of uncritical acceptance, made many thinkers abandon their customary non-involvement in matters political. Just like the young rebels of a later day, the intellectuals acted spontaneously rather than from a preconceived platform. Recognising the danger of a population in mental isolation, they blamed the government for making no effort to change that state of affairs.

Change, improvement, enlightenment and mental revolution were the demands those men made of a people wishing to keep up with the advanced nations in the age of space flight. They propagated these ideas in the press, in books and television features. Necessarily, their activity drew them much closer to the opposition camp.

To the SPD and its chairman, the movement was above all a confirmation of their policy. At the extraordinary Godesberg party conference in February 1964, where he was elected chairman as *primus inter tres,* Willy Brandt opened his speech by quoting Kurt Schumacher : "Neither regarding ideas nor persons are we conservative. The fact that our all-over political design has been justified by history does not close our eyes to the need to re-evaluate much and to employ many new means in our fight." Brandt then made a statement that encouraged the intellectuals to make common cause with his party. He said : "We have developed the new-style, forward-looking people's party ... In order to get our people to move and lead it forward, we must keep on the move ourselves. . . ."

Any sign of revolt against the ruling system on the part of the intellectuals made them appear to be left-wing. Willy Brandt commented : "It is only natural for the intellect to tend slightly towards the left. Not in the sense of dusty old slogans but in the original sense of the French Revolution. It is no coincidence that under President Kennedy artists and scientists were called into the White House."

Chancellor Erhard responded rather uncharitably to the intellectual challenge, thus rallying the mental elite more than ever against his party.

Twenty four writers joined forces in their support of Brandt and the Socialists. A remarkable book, entitled *A Plea for a New Government,* was edited by Hans Werner Richter, with support by Günter Grass and Playwright Rolf Hochhuth who had become famous through his stage success *The Representative.* Robert

Willy Brandt with Novelist Günter Grass

Willy Brandt with Novelist Martin Walser

Willy Brandt and Sir Frank Roberts Signing
the 1967 German-British Currency Agreement

Willy Brandt and Charles de Gaulle

Havemann, who had recently escaped from East Germany where he had held a prominent position, was still a controversial figure in the West and may have hindered the movement rather than helped. Yet a very apt summary of German society came from the pen of Peter Weiss of *Marat-de Sade* fame, who wrote, invoking the analogy of Schlaraffenland, the German version of cloud cuckoo land :

"The social democracy you planned lies buried under the big candy mountain. Although the place where fried pigeons fly is now all agog with surprise, I still see none but sleepers in the candy; they lie there smacking their lips and snoring and chewing the cud in their sleep; and if a voice calls out : Brothers and sisters, all is well, you shall continue to be guided towards your fortune, they will sleepily murmur hurrah, roll over on their sides and go on slumbering ... why, they would surely go on sleeping the sleep of the just beside the hydrogen bomb, were they to get it."

The emerging intellectual revolt was not of Brandt's making. He freely admitted having talked with the writers. "Some of them live permanently in Berlin, others intermittently. Grass, Richter, Johnson are there; in fact, one can hardly avoid meeting them. As mayor I must speak to everyone. The rest is easy. The intelligentsia has not always been treated well in this country. I want to help improve the climate. Emile Zola said that a writer's genius was his courage. It seems to me there must be courage also for commitment."

Günter Grass, the novelist, for one was serious about his commitment. Neither in 1965 nor in the next election year, 1969, was it show business when he rode across the land in a minibus full of election stickers of his own device to support the Social Democrats out of his own pocket and at his own risk. Eager for confrontation, he tackled places where the government parties had long been entrenched, earning laughter and derision but also leaving many of his listeners thoughtful.

The CDU and CSU people treated Willy Brandt as though it was his fault if members of the intelligentsia went canvassing for his party.

In the *Kabaretts* of West Germany election feelings ran equally high. These cabarets are a typically German institution, a kind

39

of small stage featuring political satire. The Esso slogan, Put a Tiger in your tank, was adapted to exhort the voters to 'Put Our Willy in Your Tank', and there were similar slogans of equal mass appeal.

Within the SPD the idea of an all-out fight to make it in 1965 had taken hold. At the party congress in Bad Godesberg, Willy Brandt had coined a new motto: "Our goal for 1965—the SPD shall be the strongest party."

At the same congress he said: "We've just got to win. Then it will be easier to talk. If anyone thinks we want to hug the CDU out of its breath, he is mistaken. Why should we? One hugs people from love or from hostility. The way we see it, the Christian Democrats deserve neither. At times one may even feel sorry for them since Adenauer is gone—We want no pointless or even venomous party strife."

In that election year speakers of every party made much of the number twenty. And for a good reason, for it was then twenty years since a disastrous war and a criminal dictatorship had come to an end, leaving the German people and its country both externally beaten and internally disunited and exhausted.

Now, a score of years later, the people of West Germany were once more being asked to cast their democratic ballot for the government of their choice. Brandt sought to bridge those two decades when he declared:

"Twenty years are enough. Enough rift, enough resignation, enough looking back. The German nation has not forgotten the grim lesson of its history. But it looks ahead—to a future which must offer our people the same rights as it offers other peoples."

It was still holiday time in affluent West Germany. The Mestekötters of Westphalia had flown down to Lido di Jesolo. Parked on the camping site in Antibes was the caravan of the Messmers of Saarlouis. The Struwes of Hamburg were holidaying in Wallgau near Mittenwald, while the Übelackers of Nürnberg were acquiring their tan on the Black Sea shore at Constanza. Seven million German families were for the moment preoccupied with matters other than SPD, FDP or CDU.

But those who had stayed at home were being canvassed. 28 Hardenberg Street, Berlin-Charlottenburg was the address that issued the Socialist Party slogans. The staff of 'Willy's election office' comprised a number of literary men who were busy thinking up election slogans like 'Overtake Safely on the Left—Vote SPD'; 'Stay with Your Wife, but Change Your Party' and 'He Lives in Berlin and Thinks for Germany : Willy Brandt'.

Once again Berlin was an asset to Brandt. He wanted to enter the campaign with the issue of the city and its problems. In addition he would come equipped with his party's arguments which he believed to be the more telling ones. He wished to start early, reasoning that the people would be absorbed by their own affairs once the holiday season ended. Brandt intended to make some 550 speeches, not planning a 'marathon of abuse', nor 'gentle persuasion', but speaking "clearly and plainly and straightforwardly and, where necessary, even with objective sharpness".

The press reported on Brandt's 'tour of tribulation' :

"Willy Brandt is the first to have entered the hustings. At Bonn's *Bundeshaus* he faced the press—tanned, rested and slimmer. The SPD chairman, governing mayor of Berlin and shadow Chancellor knows that the next few weeks of parliamentary electioneering mean now or never. He is facing a cross-country tour without example; a 'tour of tribulation! of which he will not know before the evening of September 19 whether it has been worth it.

First leg: Hesse ... August 10 : On through Upper Bavaria. Next day a tour of towns and villages on the Bodensee.

Brandt's trip included inspecting factories, visiting ladies' afternoons, local band concerts, socials, delivering short addresses and holding press conferences. The publicity agents and election managers called it 'charming the voters'.

The Chancellor candidate travels in a special train, consisting of a day coach, a sleeping car, a first-class coach, an office coach harbouring his store of election material and a carrier with two blocked-up Mercedes cars for brief road trips.

In the closing phase of the campaign a second sleeping car will be added for the journalists joining the tour.

Also of the party is Brandt's middle son, Lars. The fair-haired sixteen-year-old accompanied his father to Bonn because "I want to hear what questions people ask Father". After the press conference he remarked : "The questions did not surprise me at all. Father expected them and was well prepared."

41

August 14: all-German SPD meeting in Dortmund. To the Socialists, the signal for the campaign's end spurt.

"My party and my team have more in our knapsacks," said Brandt. The luggage he was alluding to was the pledged transformation of education and training, research and health policy, modernised communications and a revamping of towns and cities. "If Chancellor Erhard speaks of the necessity of solving communal problems it does not sound convincing. Those who have ruled in Bonn for 16 years had better explain why certain tasks have not yet been tackled."

The courtship of the voters has risen to a feverish pitch. The Mercedes 300 sports a standard featuring the bear in a white field (Berlin's emblem). 44 big cities and hundreds of smaller places are on the itinerary.

"There he is!" just after 2 p.m. a crowd of Bottrop citizens raise their faces to the sky, as a helicopter slowly descends from the grey rain clouds. Minutes later Brandt climbs out, waving to the crowd before getting into his car. Applause, martial music, the strains of the inevitable *'Berliner Luft'* (Berlin Air) which has come to be something of a signature tune for the world's most famous mayor. Banners bearing slogans; a local party official shouting over the heads of the crowd: "We salute the future Federal Chancellor!"

The helicopter is Brandt's advantage over Ludwig Erhard who conducts his campaign by train and motor car alone. At a charge of 450 marks an hour, the helicopter rushes Brandt back to his team after attending Bonn conferences or paying flying visits to more remote places.

If the 1961 campaign had stood in the sign of 'Smiling Willy' modelled on President Kennedy's person, the image presented in 1965 was a different one. The Chancellor candidate appeared more sure of himself, he was quieter and more dignified. Even his opponents had to admit that he cut a better figure.

His election managers had worked hard. Everything was planned down to the minute; and Brandt stuck closely to his schedule. He must not be late for punctuality was his virtue.

The column of election cars, with the loudspeaker van at its head, was directed through suburbs and housing estates to present the candidate to people who do not normally attend election meetings, such as housewives, old-age pensioners and people who were just out for a walk. The woman's vote was of special importance, it had decided many an election.

Rain was falling in the Ruhr, yet thousands were lining the streets and squares. Brandt apologized : "I am sorry I have not been able to bring you sunshine. I am afraid I cannot change the weather, but I can change a lot of other things ..." That sort of remark never failed.

In the evening there were usually three or four major meetings, either indoors or in city parks. In Hagen a crowd of some 10,000 stood closely packed, in Iserlohn the Parkhalle was full to overflowing.

Was Willy Brandt's road clear? Strangely enough, by the time of his bitter defeat of September 19, 1965, his future victory had been pre-ensured; before long he would enter the Grand Coalition, to step out on his own in 1969.

During the 1965 campaign an uncommitted, unemotional school-mistress noted : "When he arrived we were surprised at his natural and simple manner. He rejected clever oratory and asked for better understanding." It was that air of absolute integrity and the very absence of smooth election talk that contributed much to Brandt's credibility.

For a few more days, Novelist Grass kept up his one-man campaign on behalf of the SPD. "There are two private citizens," he said, "travelling in the election campaign. Both think it would be a misfortune if Chancellor Erhard continued his leadership. One is Konrad Adenauer, the other is me."

Four days before election day, Brandt was highly optimistic, counting on the greatest success in the history of his party. At a press conference in Bonn he said that thanks to the SPD's efforts, crucial inner-political questions had become election issues. The campaign had shown that government, coalition and CDU were at bigger loggerheads than ever.

Brandt's election team had provided him with arguments, had made observations and conducted public opinion polls. Brandt had them in mind when he observed in his last speech in Bielefeld : "The latest surveys show that we are leading by a nose, possibly because our opponents have so often turned back their noses."

As sometimes happens, too much faith was placed in demoscopic surveys. The campaign managers took them too seriously, instilling in Brandt unwarranted hopes of victory.

On the eve of election day, Brandt and his family had gone to the Hebbel Theatre in Berlin. The play they saw was *The Clairvoyant,* an ironic title in view of the next day's events.

For by midnight every shred of hope had been destroyed, though friends and sympathisers had clung to their optimistic estimates to the last. Vexation, exhaustion and disappointment marked the mood of that bitter hour.

As Others See Him

"Willy Brandt is a sincere and honest man," said Charles de Gaulle. "Willy Brandt is not a hypocrite. He hides nothing and he has nothing to hide," wrote Golo Mann. "For years I tried to find a symbol in Germany that I would be able to hold on to. Now I can hold on to Willy Brandt," confessed Marlene Dietrich.

From the time Brandt became governing mayor of Berlin in 1957, the world had accorded him respect and esteem. His name became a household word. "His popularity," wrote *Christ und Welt,* the Stuttgart weekly, "can easily compare with the Volkswagen's."

As early as 1960 the *Washington News* had called Brandt "one of postwar Europe's most dynamic and exciting young men." Bernd Conrad, correspondent of the influential weekly, *Die Welt,* had written : "After his visit to President Kennedy, Washington lies at Willy Brandt's feet, something that does not happen to a politican every day."

The late gossip columnist, Elsa Maxwell, wrote in the *New York Times :* "When I first saw Willy Brandt and talked to him I knew : Here is the new German Chancellor ! He would not believe me then, but today, after his visit to the White House, I know how right I was." Right she was indeed, although she missed her guess by eight years.

When Brandt had become Foreign Minister, Robert F. Kennedy said to him : "You know, I can't get used to your new title ; I guess I'll go on calling you Governing Foreign Minister."

Novelist Erich Maria Remarque wrote to the new Foreign Minister, saying : "To Germany's good fortune, you have accepted your new office. By doing so you have given everyone who really cares for Germany a feeling of security. And that security no one

45

but you was able to provide. We are grateful and happy that you have done so."

Journalist Johannes Gross called Brandt "the most effective Foreign Minister that Germany ever had".

After Brandt's election to Federal Chancellor, heaps of telegrams and letters piled up at Palais Schaumburg, at SPD headquarters and at his private address. Statesmen and heads of government, diplomats of every nation and notable personalities from both home and abroad, as well as thousands of 'nameless' citizens had sent messages of congratulation.

"All our good wishes on your election as Chancellor," wired Publisher Kurt Desch. "A new era has begun for Germany." "October 21, 1969, is the most auspicious day for democracy in Germany since May 8, 1945," wrote Playwright Rolf Hochhuth. The 'Ships Pilots' Union Elbe' sent a telegram, saying: "As the new pilot of our ship of State we wish you God Speed and a steady foot of water beneath your keel."

In *Vorwärts,* Herbert Wehner wrote: "As Chancellor, Willy Brandt will serve our people honestly and in an exemplary fashion."

The 'Governing Foreign Minister'

"The SPD chairman as German Foreign Minister in Paris in December 1966—who would have thought it possible only six weeks ago? I sometimes have to pinch my arm to make sure it's true."

Klaus Schütz
the present governing mayor of Berlin, then Secretary of State at the Foreign Office

"I feel it is an irony of history that a Social Democrat had to become German Foreign Minister in order to stop the German Gaullists from causing you trouble."

Willy Brandt
to President de Gaulle in December 1966

On the night of the election defeat of 1965 Brandt did not think ahead to the future. Despite the *Clairvoyant,* he could not have done so, had he wished. For the moment he was busy brooding over that second lost battle. The signs had proved false; the voters had turned against him, their majority at any rate.

If Brandt thinks back about that night he knows that things were looking bleak indeed. At SPD headquarters that night, the journalists saw irritable men and gloomy faces; they saw bitterness and disillusion, heard a note of uncertainty in shaking voices. Understandably, for these men had staked everything on finally beating the Christian Union.

However, neither Willy Brandt nor his party could afford to remain inactive on account of the pain of failure.

On September 20, 1965, the familiar blue-lettered bulletin went out from SPD headquarters in Erich-Ollenhauer Street, its masthead

47

reading: Editor, Herbert Wehner; Staff Editor, Franz Barsig. It was Vol. 579/65 and concerned the election results. Its opening paragraph read: Presidium and shadow cabinet of the Social Democratic Party met in Bonn on Monday, September 20, to confer about the outcome of the national election ...

Bonn-accredited newspapermen were further told that "the Social Democratic Party of Germany failed to meet its election goal of becoming the biggest fraction in the German *Bundestag*. However, the party managed to convince more than 12.7 million voters of the rightness of its policy. Compared with the last national election there has been a gain of 1.4 million votes ...

"Both Presidium and shadow cabinet wish to extend their thanks to SPD chairman Willy Brandt who scored a major achievement and convinced the electorate wherever he appeared.

"The CDU/CSU did not achieve an absolute majority. Nonetheless, they are the election winners, although it must not be overlooked that the present government coalition has lost 15 seats. The SPD has recorded a steady if slow upward trend.

"The SPD will continue to pursue and develop its policy.

"The election has failed to settle any factual issues. Not having succeeded in doing so in the last four years, the CDU/CSU will have to prove whether the election results enable them to settle them now. This applies both to the Federal Republic's difficult international position and to the unsolved problems of internal policy ..."

That the mood and situation of the Socialists and their chairman were not exactly rosy in those late September days was obvious even to outsiders. The gravest shock perhaps was the fact that not even the 40 per cent mark had been exceeded. And even Fritz Erler, whom some party people would have favoured as shadow Chancellor candidate, had met with a crushing defeat, having been beaten for the third time in his constituency.

Willy Brandt needed time to get over his defeat. On the Wednesday evening following the election he gave a press conference in which he pointed out how deeply he had been hurt by the "dirty election campaign" waged against his person. "I have not escaped unscathed from that campaign," he declared, adding that the experience would not prevent him from continuing his work for the internal reconciliation of the German people.

48

The day after appears to have marked the turning point for Brandt and his party. The governing mayor—as Brandt still called himself officially—returned to Berlin and immediately attended a session of the Municipal Assembly at which the budget bill for 1966 had its first reading. On entering the house, Brandt was greeted with lively applause by his friends and sympathisers in the gathering.

By his appearance at that session, Brandt provided the answer to the question of what conclusion he had drawn from his election defeat. The party presidium respected his wish to remain governing mayor. Incidentally, he had announced even prior to the election that he would retain that office in case of defeat.

Brandt had once more found his feet. No longer did resignation cloud his view of the future. In his mind, his party's future policy was already assuming shape. He submitted six points to the government, stressing the many problems that the coalition must now re-appraise in view of the large SPD fraction. He emphasized that the Union parties must now make good their election pledges, especially those regarding war victims and refugees. There was going to be a close scrutiny of the budget and of measures to maintain price stability. An amendment of the Constitution would not be possible without SPD approval. Finally, the SPD chairman called for plain speaking about foreign and inter-German policy: "The disunity within the coalition is no excuse for the obfuscation of issues relating to both foreign and inter-German policy."

Yet there was also a hint of resignation as Brandt announced: "The office of Chancellor candidate has ceased to exist in the SPD. I shall serve my party best by giving up my candidacy for 1969." Yet there was nothing against combining his job of governing mayor with the chairmanship of his party, since Berlin was a part of free Germany and was not situated "somewhere in Siberia".

During the next few weeks Willy Brandt experienced a grave health crisis as well as turbulent days in the Berlin party organisation. However, he had to surmount both without hurting feelings on either side. At the end of October, back from a holiday and looking tanned and rested, he made his first speech since the election before his most faithful followers, the Berlin party functionaries. "I did not leave the scene as a man bankrupt," he told his audience, perhaps on an apologetic note in view of the recent past. But under the waves of applause from the floor, the old Willy Brandt soon re-emerged, for here, among his loyal friends, he could afford to drop the campaigning politician's mask.

The hour's first priority was to restore order in the party's ranks in Berlin, where as non-voters one had followed events from a different angle. A rather harsh controversy had to be settled on whether the party's course should be steered towards the right or the left. The chairman's speech, planned as just one of the meeting's features, turned into a full evening's one-man show. When it was over, there was relief and delighted slapping of backs. "Didn't I tell you?" old party members laughed. "We've made a comeback, man! Our Willy's back in top form." If the start of the evening had seemed to confirm the rumours about Brandt being 'a broken man', any worry on that score had been dispelled. His confidence had returned under his followers faith in his leadership. Those two hours of speaking with hardly a glance at his notes had made all talk of resignation a thing of the past. Nor could Brandt's third time candidacy for the Chancellorship have been entirely abandoned that night, even if he thought so. For no one in the land could then have guessed how radically and completely the situation would change within a year.

Brandt had no inkling of what was to come when he reviewed the situation in the party press service four days before Christmas : "The year 1965 did not consist of only one day, September 19. There was not only one decision, the election decision. Social Democrats at the federal, regional and local level have shouldered much new responsibility and various new commitments. We have not departed from our road, even if we have occasionally had to move to its verge if that was the place where something could be done for the people." Brandt went on to say that the party had made good progress during the year and that after all each year brought new opportunities. What 1966 would bring was largely up to the Socialists themselves. "Not the fundamental 'no' of the unimaginative but the bold 'yes' to Germany's future must be the basis of our political credo."

Early in 1965 attempts had been made to arrange for Brandt, Wehner and Erler to address public meetings in Karl-Marx-Stadt,

Willy Brandt with Marshal Tito and the Marshal's
Wife   Jouvanka

Willy Brandt at the Reception Given by Soviet Ambassador
Tsarapkin on the 50th Anniversary of the October Revolution

Willy Brandt as Governing Mayor of Berlin, and Frau Brandt,
returning from President Kennedy's Funeral

Willy Brandt and Frau Brandt at the Bonn Press Ball

the former Chemnitz, while East German politicians were to speak to the West German public in Hanover. For several weeks the ensuing tug-of-war about the East-West exchange of speakers kept the whole country in suspense.

The possibility of establishing contact with the population beyond the Berlin Wall was discussed in a Bonn meeting consisting of *Bundestag* members of all parties, where Brandt emphasized that the three SPD representatives would be speaking on behalf of all West German democratic forces.

Ulbricht evidently wished to appear as democratic as the West Germans. In any case, he expressed his initial approval of such an exchange of speakers. But no sooner had he managed to put himself in the limelight than he saw to it that the date was postponed. Discussions began about safe conduct for the East German speakers, since Federal German law called for their arrest upon stepping on West German soil in case they were responsible for any shots fired at the Berlin Wall.

In May, Brandt still thought it possible to find a way out of the dilemma as all West German parties had agreed that an exchange of speakers would be worth striving for.

However, nothing came out of the matter, and no SPD speaker appeared in Karl-Marx-Stadt or any other East German city that year.

The Dortmund SPD party conference in June 1966 marked the big turning point for both the SPD and its chairman. There was a minority of members still clinging to old-style, emotional socialist ideas. Though largely outnumbered, they did their best to sway their more forward-looking colleagues in a desperate attempt to brighten up the dusty image of the old blue-collar, cloth-cap days.

As the outburst died down in the Dortmund hall, Herbert Wehner sat down again at the Presidium table. Blue smoke clouds were rising from behind the cardboard sign bearing his name. His 'obligatory' speech about a term of probation for the party had met with applause, but not from everyone. Wehner had called the nay-sayers 'jack-o'-lanterns' because of their intransigent stand against the SPD's attitude to the emergency laws. However, after Wehner's speech that minority of 40 out of 340 had to recognize that they were beaten. At that point, Socialist Radke of Hesse, legal assistant to the powerful trade union boss, Brenner, turned loose an incendiary bomb by hinting boldly that it might amount to the writing on the wall if the partnership between Social Democrats and trade unionists were to founder after a century.

Willy Brandt rushed to the platform to put out the flames. Speaking with greater force than in the previous day's declaration of his party's policy for Germany, his voice held a note of ringing conviction as he gave his unequivocal decision on the party's future.

But there was yet another incident that night. Fritz Erler had made a point of reproof when, like the crack of a whip, a shout of "slanderer!" rang through the hall. For moments the scene was almost eerie; Erler's face turned white; not a sound could be heard in the hall. Then, suddenly, a storm of support broke loose, wiping out every trace of defiance before it could take root.

In Dortmund Brandt emerged victorious; two days later came his first major post-election success, when he was re-elected chairman by 324 votes out of 326. Taken by surprise, he stepped up to the microphone : "This trust placed in me," he said, "confers a distinction and an obligation. I am grateful." It was a ballot such as even the legendary Socialist August Bebel had never achieved.

There may have been doubt and disunity before, but now all that was forgotten. Already the first astute commentators suggested that the SPD had not only emerged from Dortmund as the leaders of a new initiative for a united Germany but had a new and polished Chancellor candidate in Willy Brandt.

Before the SPD could even have had a chance to jeopardize its relationship with the German Democratic Republic, thereby running counter to the people's feelings in their ever wakeful mistrust of all things East German, Ulbricht's propaganda chief, Albert Norden, made a longwinded speech that let the cat out of the bag. The GDR had made overtures to the Social Democrats in the hope of turning them against the West German government's internal and foreign policy. Norden said that much quite clearly : "To defend the CDU policy one does not need a German dialogue." Norden also accused Brandt of approving and supporting the "Bonn imperialists' preparations for annexion and war". He alleged that the SPD was fully informed of the *Bundeswehr*'s "war plans" and indeed endorsed them.

The target of these accusations regarded East Berlin's conduct as a regression to the Cold War. "I do regret this decision," he remarked. "But I hope that the world will not take such attempts at distortion and defamation seriously." Brandt criticized Norden for needing more than an hour of speaking time to come to the point which was the rejection of any open confrontation by means of free speech.

Talking at the Free University in West Berlin, Brandt also touched on the German question, saying : "If we leave matters that only we Germans can get moving alone, other countries will leave Germany alone ... I don't know whether an exchange of speakers, visitors' passes, youth and sports meetings and community contacts will get us anywhere. Things do not look good at present. But if no progress is made today, that must be no cause for triumph and I-told-you-so's, or for satisfaction in immobility ... German crises must not be treated differently from European crises or from Atlantic crises; one must investigate them and try to overcome them ..."

In the summer of 1966 the regional election campaign of Nordrhein-Westphalia was launched in which Willy Brandt was his party's star performer. Everywhere his name drew capacity crowds and induced large numbers of voters to meet the SPD candidate for regional Premier in Düsseldorf, Heinz Kühn.

Brandt had turned into a more polished and compelling speaker. His words occasionally had a cutting edge and he could drive home a point with ready wit and force.

The CDU engine had visibly run out of steam, especially in the Ruhr, where rising mountains of coal marked the recession. In the Federal Republic's most populous *Land,* or region, Erhard and his party suffered a telling blow. Overnight, Kühn had become a force to be reckoned with in Germany's most highly industrialized region.

In a way Willy Brandt was the true election winner, for without him the Socialists could not have done nearly so well. In fact, he had done a brilliant job. To be sure, it had been easier for him to fight for a cause which, though his own cause, did not involve his personal political future. On his role in the Düsseldorf election, Brandt said : "I don't exclude the possibility that we thought too hard and not always straight in 1965. But last year's events taught a lesson to us all and above all to me. After all, it is not the same if you assist a friend—in this case Heinz Kühn—as when you have to be your own salesman."

The Nordrhein-Westphalia success gave the Socialists cause for satisfaction but also for recognition of their limitations. "We cannot yet do everything we wish," said Brandt. "But the others can no longer do as they wish." For the first time the question cropped up of a grand coalition in which the Vice Chancellor's and Foreign Minister's job might go to Willy Brandt. Though usually deliberate and cautious in judging political prospects, this time Brandt needed no time to think. His clear answer was : "No."

The SPD had grown into West Germany's biggest single party. Of the 1349 seats in the eleven regional parliaments, the Socialists held nearly half—661. In noting the fact, some newspapers speculated that Brandt might stand for Federal President in 1969. The SPD party presidium issued a denial but hinted that the upward trend entitled a party which might become the strongest also in the *Bundestag* to nominate the candidate for the Presidency. Since the Free Democrats had furnished the first West German President and the Christian Democrats the second, it was felt that it should be possible for the third to be a Social Democrat.

Human lives do not proceed according to rule. Unexpected factors emerge and often result in unexpected turns of event.

To Willy Brandt, the Dortmund party conference and the Nordrhenish-Westphalian election presaged the dramatic turning point. In a matter of days, his star was once more in the ascendant in the political arena, though friends and foes had scarcely thought it possible. And then, eleven months after the crushing defeat of the 1965 election, the logical consequence of these events began to show. Brandt was predestined for high Federal office. The next few months would tell whether he would achieve it soon or not before 1969. One thing, however, was obvious. His chances better than ever, Willy Brandt was re-assuming the Chancellorship candidacy he had resigned.

On October 12, 1966, his career received a substantial boost even among groups opposing his party from the governing mayor's

Foreign Minister Brandt and Chancellor
Kiesinger at the Time of the Grand Coalition

Willy Brandt and Walter Scheel as New
Coalition Partners

Federal President Heinrich Lübke with the
Kiesinger Cabinet on December 1, 1966

Federal President Gustav Heinemann
with the Brandt Cabinet on October 22, 1969

five-hour talk with the Soviet Ambassador in East Berlin, Abrassi-
mov. Following the Ambassador's direct invitation to the governing
mayor and Frau Brandt, their black Mercedes swished ghostlike
through Checkpoint Charlie into the Eastern sector without so
much as stopping. The Soviets kept the meeting intentionally
small, with only ten persons attending. The official Bonn com-
munique said of the event : "The political part of the talk had its
climax in the discussion of general German problems related to
the present West-East situation whose topicality is rising rapidly
along with the rapidly rising topicality of West-East development.
Whether the questions discussed at the East Berlin meeting should
be the departure point for reflections on the necessity of direct
probes in several capitals should become clear in the near future."

The direct political consequences of that meeting may have
been less than stunning, yet the East Berlin talks with the Soviet
Ambassador enhanced Brandt's already substantial credibility
with the public. Indeed, it looked as if only a minor impetus was
needed to propel Brandt to a position of far greater power.

As party chairman, Willy Brandt took firm hold of the party
rudder. The top party apparatus at the Barracks in Bonn was
turned upside down, tightened up and modernised. Newcomers
advanced to important posts, some of them being entrusted with
the job of further polishing up the chief's steadily improving
image and making him still better known.

International circles without socialist affiliation were taking an
ever closer interest in the SPD's upward trend. The *New York
Herald Tribune* noted : "The SPD has excellent reasons for believing
its time has come." The paper continued that having survived
Bismarck and Ludendorff, Hitler and Adenauer, the party now
was stronger than ever and more united in domestic and foreign
policy than any other party. The election success in Nordrhein-
Westphalia had shown that 'Comrade Trend' had increased his
marching pace.

In Bonn more and more voices were calling for a grand coalition.
But Willy Brandt said early in September 1966 : "Those who
suspect us of trying to squeeze into a state of mere co-rulership
just because our strength has grown are mistaken." Wehner
concurred, adding : "We are not pushing ourselves onto the

wobbly ship of government. It would have to be rebuilt from scratch and get a different crew."

On November 10, 1966, the Socialists released a statement signed by Brandt and Wehner which was intended to introduce a new era of federal policy : "While the SPD and the FDP, which hold the majority in the *Bundestag*, have suggested in public that Professor Erhard ought to be relieved as Chancellor, the CDU/CSU fraction has expressed much the same conviction behind closed doors. The fraction ... has nominated a candidate who is to try for a majority in the *Bundestag* ... The SPD considers it necessary for the chairmen of the three *Bundestag* fractions to get together some time next week for consultations on the policy to be pursued by a new government in the interest of the country. The SPD Presidium will have an initiative to offer."

The combined votes of SPD and FDP would not have sufficed for a Chancellor election, though, for three deputies were seriously ill, among them Fritz Erler who was already marked by death.

Meetings and consultations lasting well into the small hours were a common occurrence in Bonn in those days. On November 26, Willy Brandt left the conference hall for a moment to announce that he would join the new Cabinet. The groups were now locked in the struggle for the formation of a 'limited-term partnership'.

The Grand Coalition was born, and though it was not unpopular with the public, it yet turned out in the course of the next few years not to have been the happiest solution, particularly concerning domestic policy. The FDP convened a meeting in Düsseldorf whose main theme was the party's fear of being barred from the government, thereby enhancing further the steady downward trend in its fortunes.

Thirty young Socialists went to Bonn to warn their delegates of the danger of going into coalition with the Union parties. Threatening a substantial loss in the party membership, these young men said : "You are ruining the party just as you did in 1914 ... How on earth can anyone who was in a concentration camp vote for a man like Kiesinger?"

On the other hand, the Social Democrats were just as unwilling to allow Brandt to become dependent on the FDP. A hundred different opinions were being voiced. One man, SPD deputy

Schäfer, came forward to call a spade a spade. In explanation of the party's willingness to join the Grand Coalition, he said : "If the Social Democrats join a German government after a break of 36 years, we must make sure that there is no crash landing."

In the course of the long night of November 26, the party finally quit its opposition role. At the beginning of the meeting, many a deputy still favoured the Free Democrats, but by 4 a.m. on the Sunday morning the marriage of convenience with the Christian Democrats was an accomplished fact.

Afterwards, the deputies' first concern was for their post-bags. There was not one of them who did not find telegrams from voters, friends and party organisations. With few exceptions, all said the same thing : Don't join the CDU! Nor were the senders particular in their choice of language. However, the deputies were aware that sentiment was less called for than cool and soberminded calculation.

Willy Brandt had expected the public reaction. "I should have been surprised if it had been different," he said. "This party of 720,000 active members has never been an organisation of consenters; it has always made its decisions with regard for the commitment of each member."

The new Vice Chancellor closed his talk with the press by referring to a protest meeting called in Berlin for that evening : "If I know my son Peter," he sighed, only half joking, "He will be there."

The Socialists had finally got into the government, but at first not even Brandt himself seemed very happy about it. At the Barracks he confessed to party friends : "Please believe me that I settled for a temporary 'grand solution' only after a big struggle with myself, and after discussions with competent party colleagues. This is of course no great leap forward in the country's political development, and no great leap into government authority for us Social Democrats. But it remains to be seen whether this 'grand solution' may not be a big step if it is carried out with integrity. That would at least be something."

Twice had Brandt been Chancellor candidate, twice had he failed to reach his goal. Now he was going to Bonn as the Grand Coalition's Vice Chancellor and Foreign Minister. His choice marked the less popular, personally less glamorous but in the general interest more solid and practical way. At 52, Brandt had made a decision which characterizes the man better than any attempt to interpret his attitude in various situations during his long career in politics.

Eight Socialists followed him into the Grand Coalition Cabinet. Wehner took charge of the Ministry of all-German Questions. Schiller became Economic Minister, and before long one of the best-known public figures. Trade Unionist Georg Leber was the new Minister of Communications; to Dr Gustav Heinemann went the Ministry of Justice. Hans-Jürgen Wischnewski received the portfolio for Economic Co-operation. Lauritz Lauritzen became Minister of Housing, Kate Strobel Minister of Health. Professor Carlo Schmid was put in charge of the Ministry of Affairs of the Federal Council and the *Länder*, or regions. Helmut Schmidt decided to stay in the leadership of the *Bundestag* Fraction; Alex Möller was another Social Democrat who did not desire a Cabinet post.

On December 6, Willy Brandt formally thanked his predecessor, Dr Gerhard Schröder, and assumed the post of Foreign Minister. On that occasion he spoke words which became symbolic of the new Foreign Minister's candid ways: "Those who have a sense of history will not take lightly the fact that a man of my origins and convictions has become Germany's Foreign Minister." This 'German with clean hands', as the *Daily Mirror* referred to Brandt, did not force his way into the Ministry. He had no illusions about sensational successes but knew that disappointment and enmity might be his lot.

He would maintain the general line of Germany's foreign policy with its Western orientation towards Washington and Paris. Feelers towards the East would tell if anything could be done for better relations in that direction. However, to what extent it would be possible to steer the continuity begun in 1951 under Konrad Adenauer even slightly off its course could not yet be foreseen in those early weeks.

It was typical of the free-style manners of the hard election campaign of 1969 that the Union parties should distort Brandt's efforts along those lines as treasonable to Germany. Irresponsibly parroted phrases augmented the Kremlin's fabricated arguments for establishing a new dictatorship in Czechoslovakia on August 21, 1968, suggesting that it was all due to the Federal Foreign Minister's revanchist policy.

Eight days after taking up his new duties, Brandt travelled to Paris to ratify the agreement on the continued stationing of French troops in Germany. He kept important appointments at NATO, WEU and with President de Gaulle. The French press spoke of a 'promising new beginning'. Foreign observers perceived well enough that West Germany was able to adjust to the altered situation within the Alliance only because its *Ostpolitik* won new credibility through the formation of the coalition government. It is hard to imagine that any other Foreign Minister going to Paris could have tied up such a parcel of successes there in three short days.

Less than a year later the French press and public reacted almost as if to a national disaster, when the notorious 'Ravensburg message' alleged that Willy Brandt had called de Gaulle a 'power-drunk head of State'. The German Vice Chancellor and Foreign Minister was being closely watched in both East and West and consequently that 'lapse' was widely commented everywhere. However, it quickly turned out to have been a press agency canard.

As long as government interests were at issue, the two big parties stayed 'in low gear', but in both regional and local elections the old conflicts were being aired. Nonetheless, Germany's young people could not discover any genuine policy. And while Chancellor Kiesinger became the recipient of that famous slap in the face, the Nürnberg SPD conference opened in tumult, men of ministerial rank, like Herbert Wehner and Carlo Schmid, were being subjected to rude verbal attacks, flags were burned and windows smashed.

Gradually, the Grand Coalition was drifting towards a solution : decision through elections. The autumn of 1969 would show whether the danger from both left-wing and right-wing extremist could be eliminated or not.

For the third time Willy Brandt faced the electorate as his party's candidate for the Chancellorship, this time as the top man of a government team that could with justice tell the German voters that it had the right men for the country's future policy : 'SPD—the best future you can vote for!'

And then, on September 28, 1969, the job could be done; along with the Free Democrats. For the first time since the war a Social Democrat formed a government in Germany.

A little basic arithmetic sufficed to show that there were enough deputies for the Chancellor election.

At last the long march of Willy Brandt had led to its goal, that march from Lübeck into emigration, from Berlin into the opposition and from there to Palais Schaumburg.

Yet here the politics of the seventies call for a new kind of activity. Brandt and his government believe that peace in Europe is not only the big powers' concern but that of all European countries, as well.

A hopeful beginning was the first inter-German summit. When Brandt and Stoph met in Erfurt on March 19, 1970 as representatives of the two Germanies, they were seeking to find a common platform. But even the questions of formality revealed the enormous difficulty of the undertaking. No less disappointing was the two statesmen's second meeting in Kassel, where it was possible to achieve no more than a 'pause for thought'.

However, events took a surprising turn after Under Secretary of State Egon Bahr had gone to Moscow to negotiate a renunciation-of-force agreement with the Soviet Union. The whole world was amazed to note that the Kremlin talks might produce a basis not only for Germany's conciliation with her former enemies but also for better understanding between the big powers.

And when Willy Brandt finally flew to Moscow for the signing of the treaty (see also his speech in the appendix to this book), no one could deny him or his government credit for their achievement.

Appendix : Excerpts from Brandt's Speeches

The following extracts from the most important speeches and declarations made by Willy Brandt explain the aims of his policy, and also characterise the personality of the Federal German Chancellor. World-wide response was given to the speech he delivered as Foreign Minister before he became Chancellor at the Conference of the Non-Nuclear States in Geneva on September 3, 1968.

From the Government Declaration of October 28, 1969, we have reproduced his statements on policy towards the GDR and the new guiding principles for foreign policy.

During the first meeting a Federal Chancellor has ever had with the Head of the Government of the GDR, he emphasised the obligation of preserving the unity of the German nation.

Finally we have reproduced the television speech he delivered after the signing of the German-Soviet Treaty in Moscow.

Beyond the Atomic Non-proliferation Treaty: Ways to Peace for World under Arms

Willy Brandt, Vice Chancellor and Foreign Minister of the Federal Republic of Germany, Addresses Delegates to a United Nations Conference of States That Possess No Nuclear Weapons—Geneva, September 3, 1968

I

This assembly hall has been a witness to many hopes and many disappointments of the nations between two world wars. It is the home of a conference which by its nature and purpose can even today be called historic, for one thing, because an overwhelming majority of states are meeting here to seek their common interests in spite of different social systems, political standpoints, and other shades of orientation. What unites us all is the will to forego the atom as a weapon.

What unites us all is also the conviction that this self-imposed restriction must not lead to any degradation of our nations, but that it must serve the peace and advancement of mankind.

This conference can also be termed historic, because it makes us realise that it is not sufficient to prevent atomic chaos in order to ward off the dangers to the independence of states and inviolability of their sovereignty. There is no evading this experience.

The states that do not possess any nuclear weapons wish to know how they can obtain more security. They want to discuss how the arms race can be limited and brought under control in order to make peace more secure.

This is not an academic subject. We cannot solve these problems in thin air, but only with our feet firmly on the ground, in the reality of the world we live in.

Without confidence in certain fundamental rules of the common existence of states there can be no control of the destructive forces inherent in nuclear energy. Unless there is such confidence there can be no international order. Signatures are worth nothing if they are not based on a minimum of reliability.

Whoever possesses power, and especially nuclear power, does not necessarily have morality on his side, nor wisdom. To me the task of this conference is not to organise unproductive resistance against those world powers; on them history has placed a gigantic burden of responsibility, which I do not envy them.

The great dangers to mankind emanate from great powers, not from small ones. In other words, it will also be necessary to define the obligations to which the nuclear-weapon states have to submit themselves.

It would be sheer madness were we to strive to acquire the same destructive potential for all. But it is reasonable and necessary to try to achieve that equality of rights and opportunities for all states without which we cannot face our peoples, nor the younger generation, nor history.

My delegation have not come here for any other purpose than to make a positive contribution. For the cause of the peaceful use of nuclear energy we extend our hand in partnership and co-operation. In the question of security we wish to participate in efforts to come closer to positive results.

Everyone in this assembly hall knows that the threat of force and fear of force are not abstract matters. Everyone knows that nations fear for their independence and that there is deep concern for the future of mankind.

The rules of international co-existence and the work of restoring mutual trust that appeared to have been achieved, inspite of setbacks, in the years after the Second World War—all that is once again at stake.

No matter what one may understand by the sphere of interests of a great nuclear power, it does not alter the fact that the universal rules of general international law that are also bindingly embodied as principles in the United Nations Charter, and remain unrestrictedly valid, must not be violated. Those principles are sovereignty, territorial integrity, non-violence, the right of self-determination of nations, and human rights.

We shall not be able to discuss security guarantees, disarmament, and the perspectives for the peaceful use of nuclear energy with any prospect of success unless a common will and joint proposals put right the rules of order which the community of nations urgently needs.

The progress and the outcome of this conference will, logically, determine how the states assembled here will continue their work.

II

The Federal Government has given an undertaking to its allies not to manufacture nuclear weapons and has subjected itself to appropriate international controls. It does not seek any national control over nuclear weapons nor national possession of such weapons.

It reaffirms that position. Its security lies in an alliance. At the same time, being one of the non-nuclear states, we identify ourselves with the general demand for the non-use of pressure and of the threat of force.

It is still a long way from the Security Council resolution of June 19, 1968, and the declarations by the three nuclear-weapon states related to it, as well as from the non-use of force contained in the last sentence of the preamble to the non-proliferation treaty, to a well-balanced security system.

Let us be realistic. As long as nuclear weapons are not universally abolished, they cannot be eliminated as a means of deterrence and collective self-defence.

It is obviously not enough to ban nuclear aggression or the threat of it in order to safeguard the security interests of the non-nuclear states and to comply with their legitimate desire to develop in dignity and independence. There is no doubt that a nuclear state can endanger the security and independence of a non-nuclear state by using conventional weapons; there would not even be any need to threaten to employ its nuclear potential.

Hence the demand that states should mutually undertake not to use force: the non-nuclears against each other and the nuclear powers against the non-nuclears. The only legitimate exception would then be the right to individual and collective self-defence pursuant to Article 51 of the United Nations Charter.

Only a general prohibition of force admitting no other exception, which is one of the principles contained in the United Nations Charter, can be conducive to peaceful relations between states; it is therefore not admissible to confine the renunciation of force to specific states.

As far as we are concerned, I would add that we concede to no one the right of intervention.

The question arises whether the overriding principle of the renunciation of force is not the indispensable criterion on which this conference could base a resolution or a convention on the security of the non-nuclear-weapon states.

The German delegation are prepared to submit their own proposals and to help in the elaboration of pertinent proposals made by others.

We will try to achieve a prohibition of any aggression with nuclear, biological, chemical and conventional weapons, as well as of the direct or indirect threat of such an aggression, as a breach of the generally valid principle of non-violence that is also laid down in the principles of Article 2 of the United Nations Charter.

The renunciation of the use and threat of pressure and force, in any form, which might menace the territorial integrity and political independence of states should be generally renewed. States should reaffirm their obligation to shape their international relations on the basis of sovereign equality and the self-determination of peoples and to settle by peaceful means any differences that may arise.

They should agree upon the greatest possible measure of international co-operation with the aim of implementing the principles of the United Nations Charter in the fields of disarmament and arms control, thus taking a step to free mankind from fear.

The Federal Republic of Germany welcomed the treaty on a nuclear-free zone signed by the Latin American countries just as much as the decisions taken by the Organisation of African Unity which could lead to a nuclear-free zone in that continent, too.

Europe is not in the happy position of being free from nuclear weapons. It will be a hard task, and one that cannot be solved quickly, to remove existing nuclear weapons without dangerously changing the overall balance of power—in other words, by taking into account the security interests of all concerned.

The Federal Government has advocated that Europe should be made into a zone of détente as a preliminary step towards a lasting peace arrangement. It has proposed the elimination of confrontations, reciprocal renunciations of the use of force, normalisation of relations with the countries of Eastern and Southeastern Europe, a *modus vivendi* in Germany, and facilitated exchanges in the cultural, economic and scientific fields.

These efforts have now been dealt a severe blow.

We are nevertheless still prepared to work for a "European zone of peaceful neighbourliness", which would gradually lead to constructive co-operation and in which the dangerous confrontation can be diminished.

We therefore continue to support a balanced, mutual reduction of troops, which could go hand in hand with an appropriate settlement of the problem of the nuclear weapons stationed in that region.

This, incidentally, has several points of contact with the well-known Polish proposals.

In December 1967, in a speech before the German *Bundestag*, I pointed out that we are prepared to help conclude an agreement which in the course of a balanced reduction of all armed forces would also lead to a step-by-step decrease of nuclear weapons in the whole of Europe. This we are still prepared to do.

I do not wish to hide the fact that in the present world situation my government can look upon security measures in the form of resolutions, declarations or conventions only as supplementary supports for its security. The world must succeed in removing the major causes of the insecurity of the non-nuclears step by step—in other words, to press on towards real nuclear disarmament together with the dismantling of the enormous potential of conventional armaments of the nuclear-weapon states as well.

The nuclear-weapon states are called upon to take concrete steps. It is up to us non-nuclear-weapon states not to relieve them of their obligations, and to support negotiable proposals for solutions.

We should also turn our attention to the removal of certain means of delivery for nuclear warheads. If it comes to negotiations on intercontinental missiles, which are what the United States and the Soviet Union have been preparing the ground for, they should also include the elimination of other long-range missiles in the whole of Europe.

When we speak of the threat of nuclear mass-destruction weapons, let us not forget that there are also other weapons of mass destruction whose effects would perhaps be even more devastating; I am thinking of biological and chemical weapons.

In 1954 the Federal Republic of Germany signed an international treaty by which it renounced the production not only of "a" but also of "b" and "c" weapons. We would appreciate it if other states were to adopt the same attitude.

The Geneva Protocol of 1925 does not define chemical and bacteriological weapons. Should the problem of "b" and "c" weapons be discussed, they should be specifically determined.

In this respect the definitions laid down when Germany renounced production in 1954 could be of value. We offer our assistance and support for all efforts aiming—without discrimination—at effectively remodelling the prohibition of "b" and "c" weapons with the object of banishing man's fear of them.

One of the main talks of this conference is to safeguard and promote the research, development and use of nuclear energy for peaceful purposes.

Freedom of research and development is the precondition for promoting the peaceful use of nuclear energy. Nobody and nothing must be allowed to impede or prevent research and development in this field. The Federal Government attaches importance to the statement on this question which the United States Government made in the United Nations on May 15, 1968.

Safeguards, too, must be strictly confined to preventing the diversion of fissionable material for nuclear-weapon purposes. This could be done by applying the principle of the instrumented safeguarding of the flow of fissionable material at strategic points. We in the Federal Republic of Germany are making considerable efforts to apply this principle.

The work we are doing in this field, in which the IAEA is also interested, is being carried out at the nuclear-research centre at Karlsruhe.

We should like to give you an opportunity of acquainting yourselves with this work on the spot. On behalf of the Federal Government, therefore, I invite interested delegates to visit our research centre at Karlsruhe, where also the modern fast-breeder technique is being developed.

Our nuclear activity is carried out within the framework of the European Atomic Energy Community. This Community has a system of safeguards that has been effectively applied for over ten years now and which will have to be retained in the event of the conclusion of a verification agreement with the IAEA.

Nuclear energy is one of the great hopes of all those nations who do not have any natural resources of their own. How else will they be able to fight mass starvation, which may develop into a catastrophe for the whole of mankind?

The Federal Republic of Germany does not intend to keep the results of its work to itself, but wishes to cooperate and share its experience with all nations. We are prepared to intensify this co-operation :

By a wider exchange of information and technical know-how, by allowing others to participate in the programmes carried out by German nuclear-research centres and research institutes, by granting scholarships and by sending experts. We wish to strengthen our present numerous contacts in every way possible and to establish new ones.

III

On September 10, 1926, forty-two years ago, Gustav Stresemann made here the speech by which he brought Germany into the then-existing community, the League of Nations. Many of the aims he proposed are still unaccomplished, the tasks unfulfilled. When today a German Foreign Minister refers to that speech, he does so conscious of the terrible price many nations and the German nation itself had to pay, because Aristide Briand's and Stresemann's warning went unheeded.

German foreign policy is exposed to much distortion and even defamation. Nobody can evade distortions entirely, but the defamations I strongly repudiate. I do this as a person whom nobody can associate with the crimes of Hitler and who in spite of this bears his share of the national responsibility.

We have learned from history.

The Federal Republic of Germany is consistently pursuing a policy which aims at establishing a peace arrangement on this continent to replace the balance of terror. There is no reasonable alternative to this.

The Germans in the Federal Republic have not sought armaments. Our federal armed forces are not a purely national army, rather they are completely integrated in the Atlantic defence alliance. There are nuclear weapons in the Federal Republic

The 'governing Foreign Minister' Willy
Brandt in his office in Bonn

Federal President Heinemann presenting to Willy Brandt
his Letter of Appointment as Federal Chancellor

Willy Brandt

of Germany, as you all know, but we do not have any control over them, nor are we ambitious to gain such control.

The Government of the Federal Republic of Germany is determined to pursue its peace policy unwaveringly and regardless of any setbacks it is not responsible for. We not only appreciate the wish of all nations to live within secure boundaries but are prepared to take this into account in word and deed—without treaties where they can be dispensed with, with treaties where they may serve the purpose.

Young people in many of our countries do not understand why we, the older ones, cannot cope with the problems of an age dominated by science. Not force, but reason alone, can give them an answer.

This is not a speech that was conceived weeks ago. It has been prepared in the past few days, and inspite of the past few days. In Central Europe there exists the largest accumulation of destructive military force there has ever been. This goes against reason. It goes against the interests of our peoples. If others demonstrate their strength and thus create new, dangerous tensions, it is not for us to reply by increasing tension.

I see it as a chance and a possibility for the non-nuclear states assembled here, and as their duty, to combine their strength of will, their strength of reason, and their strength of morality, to address an appeal to all nations and the responsible statesmen : Let every nation determine its own course, for only then will states join hands and best serve mankind which still has so many and such big problems to solve.

An Extract from the Government Declaration

Policy Towards East Germany

This Government works on the assumption that the questions which have arisen for the German people out of the Second World War and from the national treachery committed by the Hitler regime can find their ultimate answers only in a European peace arrangement. However, no one can dissuade us from our conviction that the Germans have a right to self-determination just as has any other nation.

The object of our practical political work in the years immediately ahead is to preserve the unity of the nation by decontracting the relationship between the two parts of Germany.

The Germans are one not only by reason of their language and their history with all its splendour and its misery; we are all at home in Germany. And we still have common tasks and a common responsibility: to ensure peace among us and in Europe.

Twenty years after the establishment of the Federal Republic of Germany and of the GDR [German Democratic Republic] we must prevent any further alienation of the two parts of the German nation, that is, arrive at a regular *modus vivendi* and from there proceed to co-operation.

This is not just a German interest, for it is of importance also for peace in Europe and for East-West relations. Our own attitude and that of our friends towards the international relations of the GDR depend not least on the attitude of East Berlin itself. It is, by the way, not our intention to curtail the benefits derived by our compatriots from international trade and cultural exchanges.

The Federal Government will continue the policy initiated in December 1966 and again offers the Council of Ministers of the GDR negotiations at Government level without discrimination on either side, which should lead to contractually agreed co-operation. International recognition of the GDR by the Federal Republic is out of the question. Even if there exist two states in Germany, they are not foreign countries to each other; their relations with each other can only be of a special nature.

Following up the policy of its predecessor, the Federal Government declares that its readiness for binding agreements on the reciprocal renunciation of the use or threat of force applies equally with regard to the GDR.

The Federal Government will advise the USA, Britain, and France to continue energetically the talks begun with the Soviet Union on easing and improving the situation of Berlin. The status of the city of Berlin under the special responsibility

68

of the Four Powers must remain untouched. This must not be a hindrance to seeking facilities for traffic within and to Berlin.

We shall continue to ensure the viability of Berlin. West Berlin must be placed in a position to assist in improving the political, economic and cultural relations between the two parts of Germany.

We welcome the renewed increase of intra-German trade. This has partly been due to the facilities provided by the agreement of 6 December 1968. The Federal Government considers a further expansion of these neighbourly trade relations desirable.

In conformity with its functions and responsibilities, we have changed the name of the former Ministry for All German Questions to Ministry for Inner-German Relations. Our German policy as a whole cannot be a matter for one department alone. It is a permanent responsibility for the entire Government and embraces aspects of foreign policy, of security and European policies, as much as the efforts to maintain the coherence of our people and the relations within divided Germany.

Foreign Policy and Defence

But with all this we must not forget: Only peace makes our world secure; it is only on the basis of security that peace can gain ground. This realization we share with most peoples on earth. Aware of its special responsibility in Europe the Federal Government is determined to furnish Germany's contribution towards this great aim to the best of its abilities, without overestimating the opportunities available to it.

Although we know that at present only a limited number of personnel is available for that work, we will act upon the initiative of the Federal President and co-ordinate peace research without encroaching upon the independent character of those activities. This is yet another way in which we wish to make a German contribution towards the pacification of a world torn by crises and wars. It is in the national interest to strengthen international co-operation so that peoples may better understand their environment.

The exchange of intellectual achievements is an integral part of the necessary international co-operation. In future the presentation of German civilization abroad will aim more at giving other nations an idea not only of the everlasting achievements of the past but also of the daily reality of the intellectual strife and fruitful unrest that is taking place in Germany, too, in this period of transition.

The Federal Republic of Germany will develop in a spirit of partnership its co-operation with the countries of Africa, Latin America and Asia.

On the eve of the Second Development Decade it declares: We will contribute towards a joint strategy of the burdens of development and will consider the suggestions made in the Report of the Pearson Commission. The Federal Government will endeavour to attain the aim envisaged in the Report for a public share in development aid by an annual average increase rate of 11 percent.

We will look for ways and means to make reimbursements from public capital aid fully available again for purposes of development aid.

The number of German development experts and volunteers will be increased with a view to doubling it by the mid-seventies.

69

The Federal Government will continue to improve the quality of German aid. To this end it will simplify and streamline its planning and implementation. Partnership with the countries of the Third World is not the concern of the State only. For this reason the Federal Government will also promote all non-governmental initiatives which may expedite the process of development in those countries.

The world can expect of an economically strong country such as ours a liberal foreign trade policy designed to promote the trade of all countries. We contribute towards this end by our policy and by our participation in all organizations dealing with world trade. We also intend to promote our trade with the developing countries, and here I mention but the universal preferences for commodities from the developing countries.

The foreign policy of this Federal Government follows up on the Peace Note of March 1966 and on the Policy Statement of December 1966. The policy laid down in those documents was at the time approved by all parties in the House. The will to continue and consistently develop that policy makes reiteration of it unnecessary.

The Federal Government intends to increase its co-operation in the United Nations and in other international organizations. The same applies to world-wide agreements on disarmament and arms limitations which are gaining in importance. In this respect the Federal Government will continue the policy which I, in the capacity of Foreign Minister, expounded on 3 September 1968, at the Conference of Non-Nuclear-Weapon States in Geneva.

We emphasize our fundamental readiness to have diplomatic relations and to increase existing trade relations with all states in the world that share our desire for peaceful co-operation.

The Federal Government rejects any form of discrimination, oppression and foreign rule which in our day again and again is jeopardizing the peaceful co-existence of nations.

The North Atlantic Alliance which has proved its value in the twenty years of its existence will guarantee our security also in future. Its firm solidarity is the prerequisite of joint efforts to reach a relaxation of tensions in Europe.

No matter which of the two aspects of security policy we may consider, be it our serious and continuous attempt to arrive at a simultaneous and equally balanced limitation of armaments and arms control, or be it the guarantee of an adequate defence of the Federal Republic of Germany : the Federal Government under both aspects understands its security policy as one of assuring equilibrium and peace. And it also sees under those two aspects the outward security of our State as being a function of the Alliance of which we are a member, thus contributing our share to a balance of power between East and West.

For our security we need friends and allies, just as they need us and our contribution for theirs. Without mutual confidence in the political steadfastness of that recognition neither the Alliance nor security can be maintained. We will therefore continue the present policy within and towards the Alliance, and we expect this also of our allies and their contributions towards a joint security policy and the mutually agreed joint security efforts.

Just as the Western Alliance is defensive, our own contribution to it is defensive. Neither its training and structures nor its armaments and equipment make the Federal Armed Forces suited for an offensive strategy. The Federal Government will make clear beyond any doubt that its defence policy is based upon a defensive principle.

For the Federal Government the close ties between us and the United States of America permit of no doubt that the obligations will be honoured which the United States have assumed by treaty as well as out of conviction for Europe, the Federal Republic and West Berlin. Our common interests need neither additional assurances nor repeated declarations. They are strong enough to allow for more independent German Policy within a more active partnership.

Together with its Allies the Federal Government will consistently apply itself to the task of bringing about a reduction of the military confrontation in Europe. With them it will work for a simultaneous and balanced limitation of armaments and reduction of forces in East and West.

As for the topics of a conference designed to further the cause of European security, the Federal Government reaffirms the position taken in the memorandum which was submitted in Helsinki on 12 September 1969. After careful preparation such a conference may well become an important step on the way towards more security with less armaments, and towards progress among the partners in Eastern and Western Europe.

Of the present centres of tension the conflict in the Middle East gives particular cause for alarm. The Federal Government thinks that it would be in the interests of the nations concerned to try to find a solution as offered in the Security Council's Resolution of 22 November 1967. We wish to have good relations with all states in that area, and we confirm our resolve not to supply weapons to areas of tension.

We are one with all states and also with the distressed people concerned in wishing that the war in Vietnam may at long last be ended by way of a political solution that can be accepted by all involved. We reaffirm our readiness to take part in the reconstruction of both parts of the devastated country.

European Co-operation and Understanding

Special importance attaches to the forthcoming conference of the Six in The Hague. It may well decide on whether Europe will be taking a courageous step forward with respect to the interrelated subjects of the Community's internal development, intensification and enlargement or whether it will get into a dangerous crisis. The peoples of Europe are waiting for and urging the statesmen to supplement the logic of history by the determination for success.

Franco-German accord may be decisive in this respect. The Federal Government is prepared to lend the close contractual ties that steadfastness which should serve as a model of the type of relations which can today be established between European partners.

The enlargement of the European Community must come. The Community needs Great Britain as much as the other applicant countries. In the chorus of European voices the voice of Britain must not be missing, unless Europe wants to inflict harm on herself. We are gratified to note that the decisive forces in British policy continue to be convinced that Great Britian in turn needs Europe. It is time to initiate the no doubt difficult and probably time-consuming process at the end of which the Community will find itself placed on a broader basis.

In that context the Federal Government will use its influence to help the Community develop new forms of economic co-operation with those countries of Europe which cannot or do not wish to join the Community.

The Federal Government will promote the development of a closer political co-operation in Europe with the aim of evolving step by step a common attitude in international questions. We know that in this endeavour we are in particular agreement with Italy and the Benelux countries.

Our national interest does not permit us to stand between East and West. Our country needs co-operation and co-ordination with the West and understanding with the East.

The German people need peace in the full sense of that word also with the peoples of the Soviet Union and all peoples of the European East. We are prepared to make an honest attempt at understanding, in order to help overcome the aftermath of the disaster brought on Europe by a criminal clique.

We do not harbour false hopes : Interests, power constellations and social differences can neither be dissolved dialectically nor must they be obscured. And yet our partners for talks must also realize : The right to self-determination embodied in the United Nations Charter applies also to the German nation. This right and the will to defend it are not negotiable.

We are not deluding ourselves to believe that reconciliation will be easy or quick to achieve. It is a process; but it is time now to push ahead that process.

In continuation of its predecessor's policy the Federal Government aims at equally binding agreements on the mutual renunciation of the use or threat of the use of force. Let me repeat : This readiness also applies as far as the GDR is concerned. And I wish to make as unmistakably clear that we are prepared to arrive with Czechoslovakia—our immediate neighbour—at arrangements which bridge the gulf of the past.

It is the Federal Government's firm conviction that the policy of renunciation of the use of force which respects the territorial integrity of the respective partner constitutes an essential contribution towards a relaxation of tensions in Europe. Renunciation of the use of force would create an atmosphere which makes further steps possible.

The joint efforts, too, to promote trade, technical co-operation and cultural exchange are serving this purpose.

Today the Federal Government deliberately abstains from committing itself to statements or formulae going beyond the framework of this statement, which might complicate the negotiations it desires. It is well aware that there will be no progress unless the governments in the capitals of the Warsaw Pact countries adopt a co-operative attitude.

72

Commitments to Democracy

This Government will not toady anybody. It demands much, not only of others but also of itself. It sets concrete targets. These targets can only be attained if the citizen's attitude towards his state and government undergoes change.

In a democracy a government can only work successfully if it is supported by the democratic commitment of its citizens. We are as little in need of blind approval as our people are in need of pomp and high and mighty aloofness. We do not seek admirers; we need critical people to think with us, to decide with us and to take responsibility with us.

This Government's self-confidence will express itself as tolerance. Therefore, it will appreciate the solidarity that voices itself as criticism. We are not chosen, we are elected. That is why we seek the dialogue with everyone who has this democracy at heart.

In the past years, many in this country feared that the second German democracy would go the way of the first. I have never believed this. I believe it still less today.

No: We are not at the end of our democracy, we are at its beginning. We want to become a people of good neighbours within and without.

An Excerpt from Brandt's Statement on the Erfurt Meeting

Excerpt from the Statement by Willy Brandt, Chancellor of the Federal Republic of Germany, at the Meeting With Willi Stoph, Chairman of the German Democratic Republic's Ministerial Council, March 19, 1970, in Erfurt

Mr. Chairman of the Ministerial Council; gentlemen:

The goal of this exchange of views should be to determine whether we can begin negotiations at the end of which would be contractual regulations of the relationships between the FRG and the GDR. In this matter, it is self-evident to my Government that a treaty or an accord between us must have the same binding quality that any accord would have which our Governments might conclude with third countries.

Allow me once more to state the principles that guide the Federal Government and that I mentioned to you at the time:

1. Both states have the duty to preserve the unity of the German nation. They are not foreign to one another.

2. Additionally, the generally acknowledged principles of international law must apply, particularly the exclusion of all forms of discrimination, respect for territorial integrity, a commitment to peaceful solution of all disputes, and respect for mutual borders.

3. Involved here is the commitment not to want to use force to change the social structure in the territory of the contractual partners.

4. The two Governments should strive for neighbourly co-operation, particularly in arranging for specialist-technical co-operation, joint facilitation of which can be provided for in governmental agreements.

5. The existing rights and responsibilities of the Four Powers in regard to Germany as a whole and to Berlin are to be respected.

6. The efforts of the Four Powers to reach agreements on an improvement of the situation in and around Berlin are to be respected.

Mr. Chairman, it emerges from your presentation and mine that in any case we are at the beginning of a long and wearisome road. But there can also be a second result: that, despite all which has been, and despite all that separates us, we are prepared to start on this road. We cannot ignore the things that separate us. But we should push to the foreground the questions about which an agreement might be possible.

Brandt's Television Speech from Moscow

On Wednesday evening, August 12, 1970, direct from Moscow, Federal
Chancellor Brandt delivered the following address on German
television to "all those at home in Germany"

'My dear fellow citizens,

The signing of the treaty between the Soviet Union and the Federal Republic of
Germany is an important moment in our post-war history.

Twenty-five years after the capitulation of the German Reich which Hitler
destroyed, and fifteen years after Konard Adenauer negotiated here in Moscow the
opening of direct diplomatic relations, it is time for us to lay new foundations for
our relationship to the East—those of unrestricted mutual renunciation of any
use of force, based upon the existing European political situation.

With its work on this treaty, the Federal Government has fulfilled a task it set for
itself in the Government Declaration. There it stated : "Our national interest does
not allow us to stand between the East and the West. Our country needs co-operation
and accord with the West and arrangement with the East. The German people
need peace in the fullest sense of the word, with the people of the Soviet Union,
too, and with all the peoples of Eastern Europe."

This was and still is our guiding principle, and the treaty is part of our working
for peace.

I know that I—like most of you—am not given to wishful thinking. This century—
marked as it is by blood and tears and hard work—has taught us to be sober. But this
sobriety must prove its worth especially when we are witnesses of and partners in
historical changes. We must not forget it when we have cause for satisfaction and
new hope, when we—I am not afraid of saying this are quite justified in talking
about a success.

And this treaty with the Soviet Union is a success of German post-war policy.
It is a decisive step towards improving our relations with the Soviet Union and with
our Eastern neighbours—a quarter of a century after the catastrophe which demanded
unspeakable sacrifices of the peoples in the East even more than of those in the West.

It is in the interest of the whole German people to improve our relationship
especially with the Soviet Union. It is not only one of the great world powers—
it also has its share of the special responsibility for Germany as a whole and for Berlin.

It is nine years tomorrow since the building of the wall. It is my confident hope that today we have made a beginning towards counteracting the rift, so that people will no longer have to die in the barbed-wire, until one day the division of our nation can, I hope, be overcome.

The boundary of Europe is neither the Elbe nor the Eastern border of Poland. Russia is indissolubly bound to European history, not only as an opponent and as a threat, but also as a partner—historically, politically, culturally and economically. Only when we in Western Europe can direct our eyes towards this partnership, and only when the peoples of Eastern Europe can see this too, can we come to an agreement about our interests.

With this treaty we are not losing anything that has not been gambled away a long time ago. We are courageous enough to turn over a new leaf in history. This is to benefit above all the members of the younger generation who have grown up in peace and with no responsibility for the past, and who nevertheless must bear the consequences of the war along with us, because nobody can get away from the history of his people.

This treaty in no way prejudices the firm anchoring of the Federal Republic and its free society within the Western Alliance. The reliable partnership with America will be maintained just as will be the reconciliation with France. Nor will there be any change in the firm desire to bind more and more closely together an increasing number of European states, with the aim of achieving a political community.

The treaty endangers nothing and nobody. It is intended to help to clear the way ahead. And if it achieves this, then it will further the cause of peace, of Europe and of us all.

My greetings to all of you at home in Germany.'

Facsimile of a hand written note by Willy Brandt (original size).

Publications by Willy Brandt

Ernst Reuter—Ein Leben für die Freiheit (by Willy Brandt and Richard Löwenstein)—Published by KINDLER VERLAG, MUNICH

Von Bonn nach Berlin (by Willy Brandt, Otto Uhlitz and Horst Korber)—Published by ARANI-VERLAG, BERLIN, 1957

Willy Brandt—Mein Weg nach Berlin (recorded by Leo Lania)—Published by KINDLER VERLAG, MUNICH, 1960

Plädoyer für die Zukunft (12 Contributions to German Questions)—Published by EUROPÄISCHE VERLAGSANSTALT, FRANKFURT/MAIN, 1961

Mit Herz und Hand—Published by VERLAG FÜR LITERATUR UND ZEITGESCHEHEN GmbH, HANOVER, 1962

The Ordeal of Coexistence—Published by HARVARD UNIVERSITY PRESS CAMBRIDGE, MASSACHUSETTS, 1963, AND ITS GERMAN VERSION :

Koexistenz—Zwang zum Wagnis—Published by DEUTSCHE VERLAGSANSTALT, STUTTGART, 1963

Begegnung mit Kennedy—Published by KINDLER VERLAG, MUNICH, 1964

Brandt-Reden 1961-1965 (Excerpts from the Speeches)—Published by VERLAG WISSENSCHAFT UND POLITIK, COLOGNE, 1965

Friedenspolitik in Europa—Published by S. FISCHER-VERLAG, FRANKFURT/MAIN, 1968

During the years he spent in Norway and Sweden (1933 to 1946), Brandt published a number of writings on subjects of foreign policy and current history which are in part reprinted in a book published in 1966 under the title *Draussen* (Writings of the Emigration Years) by Kindler Verlag, Munich.

Im Namen der

Bundesrepublik Deutschland

ernenne ich

auf Grund des Artikels 63 Absatz 2 des Grundgesetzes
für die Bundesrepublik Deutschland

Herrn

Willy Brandt

zum Bundeskanzler

Bonn, den   21. Oktober 1969

Der Bundespräsident

German President's decree appointing Willy Brandt as Chancellor of the Federal Republic of Germany.

Highpoints

18. 12. 1913	born in Lübeck
1931	Member of the Social Workers' Party
1932	School-leaving examinations in Lübeck
	Volunteer in a Lübeck Shipbroker firm
1933	Flight to Scandinavia
	studied History at University of Oslo
	active in journalism
1936	Expatriation
1940	German troops march into Norway
	Flight to Sweden
1942–45	Leader of Norwegian-Swedish Press bureau in Stockholm
1945	Return to Germany as Norwegian press correspondent
1946–47	Press Attache for Norwegian Military Mission in Berlin
1947	Renunciation of Norwegian Citizenship
	Return to Germany
1949–57	Social Democratic Party (SPD) Delegate to Federal Bundestag in Bonn
1950–51	Editor-in-Chief of "Berliner Stadtblatt".
1954	Chairman of Berlin SPD Representatives
1955	President of the Berlin House of Delegates
1957	Governing Mayor of Berlin
1958	Berlin Chairman of SPD, Member of the Central Committee of the SPD
1961	Candidate for Chancellor
1962	Representative Chairman of SPD
1964	Chairman of SPD
1965	Candidate for Chancellor for the second time
1966	Foreign Minister
1969	Chancellor
1970	Moscow

Index

82

L

Lauritzen, Lauritz 58
Leber, Georg 58
Leber, Julius 14, 25
Ludendorff, Erich 55

M

Mann, Golo 45
Marshall, George 26
Marx, Karl 8, 18
Maxwell, Elsa 45
Möller, Alex 35, 58

N

Norden, Albert 52, 53

O

Ollenhauer, Erich 33, 35

P

Pieck, Wilhelm 26

R

Remarque, Erich Maria 45
Reuter, Ernst 26, 27, 35, 79
Richter, Hans Werner 39

S

Schäfer, Friedrich 57
Scheel, Walter 29
Schellenberg, Ernst 35
Schiller, Karl 35
Schmid, Carlo 35, 58, 59

Schmidt, Helmut 35, 36, 58
Schröder, Gerhard 29, 58
Schütz, Klaus 47
Schumacher, Kurt 27, 28, 35, 38
Stresemann, Gustav 66
Strobel, Käte 35, 58
Suhr, Otto 28

T

Truman Harry S 26

U

Ulbricht, Walter 32, 51, 52

W

Wehner, Herbert 2, 34, 35, 46, 48, 50, 51, 55, 59
Weiss, Peter 39
Wischnewski, Hans-Jürgen 58

Z

Zola, Emilie 39